CW01302330

Dirk Schneider

Jesus Christ – Quantum Physicist

**Why modern science needs
the Trinity of Father, Son and Holy Spirit
to explain our world**

© 2015 Dirk Schneider
www.doschneider.com

Translation into English by
Brigitte Pauli-Barlos
418 Vigil Street
Taos, NM 87571, USA

All rights reserved.
No part of this book may be reproduced, scanned or distributed in any printed or electronic form without permission. Please do not participate in or encourage piracy of copyrighted materials in violation of the author's rights. Purchase only authorized editions.

Proofreading
Aimee Scott
aimee.scott26@hotmail.co.uk

Cover
Julián Fidel Marcos Llorente
info@rugbyjerseys.eu

Design, typesetting
Diana Sayegh
saydi|Design
www.saydi.de

1st Edition, June 2015

ISBN-13: 978-1511683470
ISBN-10: 1511683473

Table of Contents

1. A long nightmare begins	7
2. A case of hay fever changes the fate of the world	11
3. How to alter the course of the past	21
4. What does "eternity" mean?	29
5. Why New York is a neighboring city of San Francisco	35
6. What is omnipresence?	43
7. The most magnificent experiment of all times	49
8. What do the terms "God" and "Heaven" mean?	59
9. Does the moon exist even if no one is looking?	69
10. The secret of the Holy Spirit	83
11. Jesus Christ—the Son of God	93
About the Author	101

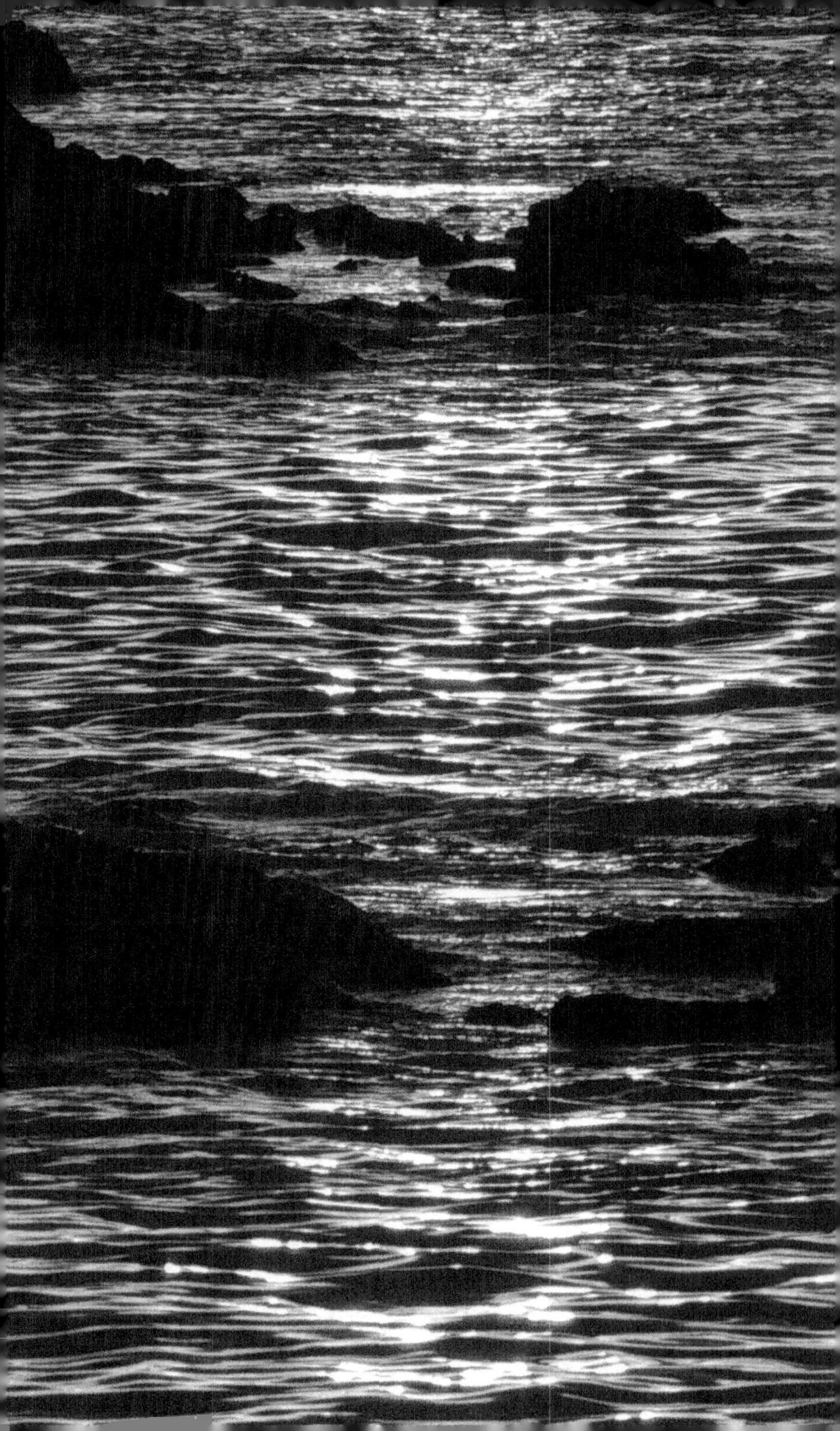

1. A long nightmare begins

Admiring and respectful eyes were upon the man as he walked down the streets of Paris. A scientist and philosopher, he had written a book on celestial mechanics, which had made him quite a celebrity—one of the most famous people of his era. In this, the early 19th century, Pierre Simon Laplace was the favorite son of the Parisian society. Many were riveted by his scientific writings packed with secrets, describing the universe and the world. In fact, even Napoleon began to take an interest and he invited Laplace to pay him a visit at the imperial palace. Legend has it that Napoleon asked Laplace during their meeting "Monsieur Laplace, how come you do not even mention God once in your book?" The author responded proudly "Well, your Majesty, why would I? In fact, I did not need this hypothesis in it at all."

Back in the day, Napoleon's question certainly seemed justified, as it was an unwritten law that God had to be mentioned at least once in any book of importance. The foundation of Laplace's five-volume work on celestial mechanics was a new era of scientific intelligence, which had been ushered in in the 16th century and reached its preliminary peak in Newton's work. According to this vision, the world is deterministic. What does this mean? Indeed, one could explain the entire scenario on the basis of the rules of pool billiards. If a billiard player taps the cue against the white billiard balls, it will eventually hit another ball, which in turn touches another one. If the initial conditions, such as the speed, the side spin (angular momentum) and the cut angle of the white ball against the first ball are known, it is possible to precisely calculate the subsequent movements of all the other billiard balls. Hence, the future would be completely predetermined by the present, just like the movements of the cogwheels in clockworks. Science currently presents us with the worldview of determinism.

In its original interpretation, determinism drew strict lines between the spiritual (mind) and the secular world (matter). In more recent times, scientists have begun to apply determinism not only to tangible but also to intangible objects. As a result the term was applied to the mind, given that the behavior of matter, which can be calculated in advance, are considered the primary cause of everything. Thoughts, emotions or morals would thus have their roots in the motions and re-grouping of nerve cells and electrons in the brain, whose behavior patterns can be calculated in advance just like the movements of billiard balls. Such a world does not offer any room for spiritual aliveness. Works of art, such as Mozart's symphonies or van Gogh's paintings would not be considered the result of artistic creativity or intuition or ideas, but that of acts that can be predicted and calculated precisely. A true nightmare.

The question is, is that really the way of the world? People thought so until 1900, when something amazing happened. An incredible revolution occurred in natural science. It came by complete surprise and did away with the prevailing worldview that had ruled until then. Unfortunately this groundbreaking change, which completely turned around the idea of what was holding the world together at its very core, happened unbeknownst to most of the human race and for most of us this is still the case today. Even though the insights this new physical theory revealed at the time provided the technical foundation for today's modern technology, we have been largely in denial of their impact on our worldviews and religion until the present time. As a consequence, most people, including many engineers and natural scientists are still attached to materialism today.

However, let's begin our journey with some time travel and go back to 1900, when the physics revolution began.

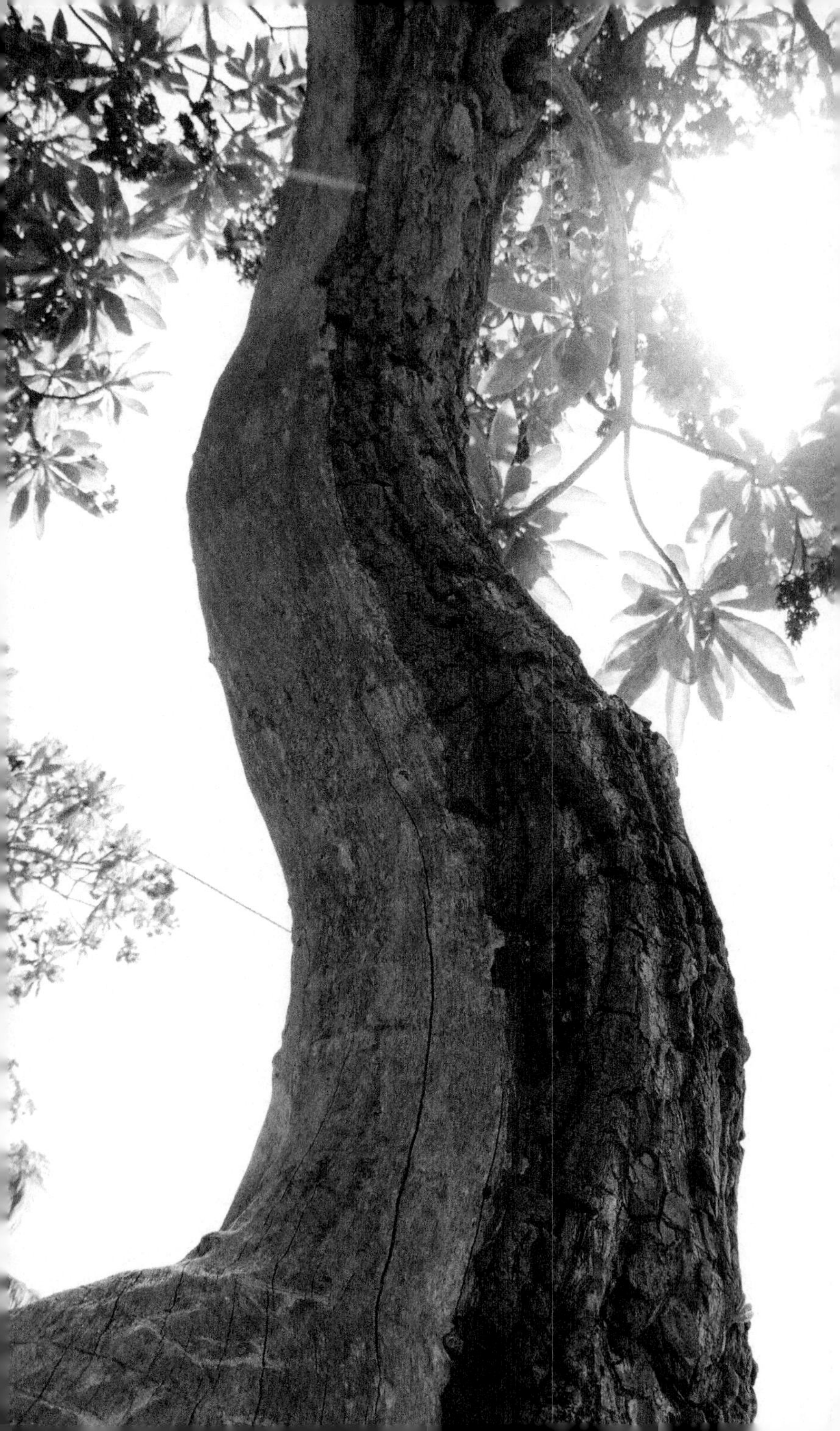

2. A case of hay fever changes the fate of the world

It was a thrilling and crazy time. Freud was out; Jung and Adler were in high demand. New artistic and architectural styles, such as the Bauhaus style, were conquering the world. Fritz Lang and Alfred Hitchcock introduced new movie production art styles through the use of a new code language. The Dadaists subjected the former standards to ridicule. Hence, the time was ripe for Dada physics that incorporated chance, irrationality and intuition as new elements. A revolutionary and completely new theory emerged, which turned the existing scientific world vision on its head.

Ironically, the foundation stone for this new approach to physics had been laid a quarter of a century earlier, by a man who was actually rather conservative and still became an unintentional revolutionary. He was already over forty when this happened. That in itself was quite unusual, since it was common for physicists to make their revolutionary discoveries at a very young age, if at all. Moreover, this man embodied the prototype persona of what people would have envisioned a typical government employee to look like back then: he wore a dark business suit, a white shirt and a black bow tie. One of his students later summed it up:

"It doesn't make any sense whatsoever that this is supposed to be the man who pursued a revolution."

The name of the man who came up with these new scientific ideas: Max Planck. The term used for his new physical theory, which was conceived in 1900: Quantum physics.

In the 1890s, while striving to give the German lighting industry a competitive edge over their British and American rivals, leading German physicists had endeavored to resolve the so-called black body problem. Their efforts did not succeed.

After a poker is heated up in the fire, it begins to glow and change its color to red and eventually to white. During this process, it radiates a mix of heat and light. Ideally, the radiation that is being generated depends only on the temperature. Under the assumption of this ideal scenario, one envisions a black and hollow container with a hole in it instead of the poker, which is referred to as the black body. After heating it up, one measures the energy radiated from the hole. Back in the day, the scientists were hoping that they would be able to measure the black body radiation to obtain a foundation for the development of better light bulbs that generated a maximum amount of light and as little heat as possible. Even today, this remains the objective of energy efficient, eco-friendly lighting.

In desperate search for a solution, Planck came up with the idea to use tiny energy packages. He called them quanta. For the solution to work light has to exist only in specific, discrete quanta of energy. This is indeed a rather revolutionary idea, given that in everyday life we are used to seeing variations of the same themes, to interim steps, to smooth transitions and shades of gray. Apples, for instance exist in many sizes and hues. If one were to apply Planck's idea to the "normal" world we live in, this would mean that there might be apples with diameters of exactly 5 and 10 cm and no sizes in between. In the context of everyday living, this whole concept sounds quite absurd. Nonetheless, it is actually one of the characteristics of the world of quantum physics.

Planck referred to his discovery as a stroke of luck. In fact, the idea had just popped into his head and had not been developed as a result of laboratory experiments. He realized that his quantum hypothesis would be the end of the worldview as it had existed until then. He made the following comment in reference to his new quantum theory:

"To sum it all up in a nutshell, I can call the entire undertaking an act of despair."

The young wild ones

Given that he was so conservative, Planck had a tough time embracing his own discovery and had faith that he would be able to restore the old physical order. He hoped in vain. The ground for the young wild ones who were ready for new ideas had been broken.

Werner Heisenberg was one of them. His birthday was December 5, 1901—almost exactly a year after Planck's revolutionary discovery. Heisenberg began his studies of physics in the summer of 1920, although he had originally planned to study mathematics. However, his application interview with one of the professors had taken a terrible turn. The professor's dog barked loudly and continuously, expressing a certain dislike. Hence, Heisenberg decided to sign up for physics instead.

He befriended Wolfgang Pauli in the early days of his student life. The two eventually had a profound impact on the progress of quantum mechanics—the mathematical description of quantum physics. Later, a supervisor referred to Wolfgang Pauli as a genius comparable to Albert

Einstein. As individuals, Heisenberg and Pauli were as different as they come, yet they were very close friends. In an excerpt from his biography entitled *Der Teil und das Ganze (The Part and the Whole)*, Werner Heisenberg describes Wolfgang Pauli as follows:

"My conversations with Wolfgang Pauli were among the most important parts of my student activities in Sommerfeld's seminar although Wolfgang's lifestyle was virtually the diametrical opposite of my own. While I loved the bright days and spent almost all of my leisure time outside of town hiking through the mountains, swimming in or grilling on the beach of a Bavarian lake, Wolfgang was an extreme night owl. He preferred being in the city, found inspiration in the evenings by patronizing amusing entertainment events at some of the local establishments and after that, would spend most of the night working with the greatest of intensity as well as success on his physics tasks. Of course that meant that to Sommerfeld's disappointment, he rarely attended the morning lectures and frequently did not even come to the seminar until lunchtime. While our different lifestyles prompted us to poke fun at each other quite a bit, it did not overshadow our friendship in any way."

Pauli, on the other hand, included the following description of Heisenberg in a letter addressed to Niels Bohr (quote from Manjit Kumar's book *Quanten (Quanta)*):

"Whenever I contemplate his ideas, they make a terrible impression on me and on the inside, I have nothing good to say about them at all. After all, he lacks a philosophical approach and he doesn't pay attention to a transparent emphasis on the fundamental assumptions and their links to previous theories. However, when I talk to him, I like him a lot and I can see that he has quite a few new arguments—at least in his heart. Notwithstanding that he as a person is also a very nice individual, I consider him very relevant—in fact, I think he is a genius and I believe that he will eventually bring a lot of progress to science."

In June of 1925, Heisenberg was in rather bad shape health-wise. He was plagued by severe hay fever. Moreover, his work at the university in Göttingen (Germany) had come to a standstill. Hence, Heisenberg decided to take a two week vacation on Helgoland, an island in the North Sea. There, he spent his time rock climbing, taking walks and reading the work of Goethe. However, he did dedicate a portion of the hours on the island to his unresolved scientific problem.

The scientists engaged in atomic physics research had been compelled to make the difficult decision to give up on the image of a miniaturized planetary system. Unfortunately, the electrons that move around the atom are not comparable to planets that circle around the sun. They have a very weird and crazy characteristic: they suddenly disappear in one location and reappear in a different one without crossing through any spaces in-between. This phenomenon is called the quantum leap.

Heisenberg came up with the idea to describe the electrons' jumps between the different tracks in some sort of table. So when he determined in the wee hours of the morning—at three o'clock to be specific—that he had apparently discovered a formula that would allow him to describe the secret of atomic processes, he was very excited and simultaneously also extremely shocked. Since he could not go back to sleep, he climbed on a rock in the south of the island to wait for the sun to rise.

However, his calculations did throw him for a loop. Heisenberg's table was contingent on a strange multiplication rule, in which a times b was not equivalent to b times a (e.g. $3 \times 4 = 4 \times 3$). This fact troubled him a lot. After his return from vacation, Heisenberg had submitted his explorations to his then-professor Max Born—who happened to be an uncle of actress and pop singer Olivia Newton John—in the form of a written thesis. Born was so impressed with Heisenberg's work that he wrote this in a letter to Albert Einstein:

"*Heisenberg's new work, which will be published soon, may look quite mystic, but it is certainly correct and thorough.*"

Thankfully, Born also had another insight. He remembered a mathematics lecture in which the matrix multiplication theory had been introduced. The rules we are familiar with, as far as the multiplication of figures is concerned, do not apply to this theory. Born drew Heisenberg's attention to this fact, who subsequently began to study this field of mathematics he had not known about until then.

The discovery: matrices describe processes and cannot be compared with regular figures. The sequence does indeed play a key role in processes. I encourage you to try it first-hand. Go ahead and close this book. Now look at the book cover and perform the following steps: turn the book to the front and then to the right (always at a 90 degree angle). Make sure to remember the positioning of the book. Repeat the entire sequence from the starting position; but in the opposite direction—turn the book to the right first and then to the front. Do you notice a difference? If you are reading the e-book version of this work, you can of course perform the same hands-on exercise with your e-book reader, tablet or smartphone.

Heisenberg's discovery revolutionized physics to such an extent that the Island of Helgoland posted a memorial plaque with the following inscription in his honor:

"In June of 1925, 23-year-old Werner Heisenberg accomplished a breakthrough in the formulation of quantum mechanics, the fundamental theory of the natural laws in the atomic field right here on Helgoland, which has had a deep impact on human thought well beyond physics."

Heisenberg's discovery ushered in a new era and within a short period of time, a vast portion of quantum mechanics was derived from his findings: The new physics of the atoms had been uncovered.

The Coen Brothers tend to elaborate on quantum physics and what the transfer of its principle to our world means for us humans in many of their movies. In *The Man Who Wasn't There*, for instance, attorney Riedenschneider is so impressed with Werner Heisenberg's Uncertainty Principle (we will talk more about this in Chapter 9) that he is confident this theory will help him prevail in an impending trial (see e.g. http://www.youtube.com/watch?v=N5RvDorEnMc). In *A Serious Man*—another Coen Brothers' film—a quantum physicist embarks on a search for God and Heisenberg's theory once again plays a central role. Of course both movies are definitely worth seeing—even if you're not keen on learning more about quantum physics.

An erotic affair

Heisenberg's introduction of the matrix formalism was a huge success. However, it had one disadvantage—it was rather imperceptible. Many physicists yearned for an alternative to this theory. A 38-year-old Austrian physicist did in fact accommodate their wishes just a few months later.

Erwin Schrödinger's educational profile was very broad: he spoke several languages and also had a keen interest in painting, music, sculpting and philosophy. Born described him as an extremely charming, amusing, benevolent and generous man. However, Schrödinger also had the reputation of quite a Casanova. He and his wife Anny were constantly pursuing affairs and did not necessarily have the kind of relationship one could have described as "civilized and proper." Just before the 1925 Christmas break, they had had another falling out, so Schrödinger wanted to get away for two weeks and seek refuge. However, before he took off, he set up a rendezvous with his paramour in Arosa, Switzerland, where he could enjoy his unfettered erotic passions without limitations. Once there, he did not only focus on his affair, but took some time to explore the field of quantum physics.

Schrödinger was intrigued by the work of a French aristocrat named de Broglie. The Frenchman postulated the wave nature of particles such as electrons and suggested that all matter has wave properties. Therefore Schrödinger wanted to know whether the electron tracks in atoms Heisenberg had depicted using matrices, could also be explained and calculated on the basis of waves.

In physics, every wave is described in what experts call a wave equation. Schrödinger embarked on a search for this concise wave equation for matter. Some authors, such as the previously mentioned Manjit Kumar, consider the time right after the Arosa vacation the most productive and innovative in Erwin Schrödinger's life. During this era he did discover the wave equation he was looking for, so his erotic affair did in fact drive him to succeed as he was still so inspired and charged with emotion.

The next question was whether he would be able to use this equation to also compute the different energy levels of the hydrogen atom. This was in fact possible with Heisenberg's matrix technique. The calculation worked, so that this alternative quantum mechanics version was published in the *Annals of Physics (Annalen der Physik)* in 1926. The wave equation was named for the man who discovered it: the Schrödinger Equation. To date, it remains the mathematical foundation of all quantum mechanics and is considered one of the most prominent equations in the history of physics.

However, one highly important question remained unresolved: what meaning did this wave have and what was moving up and down like a wave? Initially, even Erwin Schrödinger was unable to provide a satisfactory answer to this question, so his colleagues made fun of him in a poem they wrote:

Erwin with his psi can do
Calculations quite a few.
But one thing has not been seen
Just what does psi really mean.

(psi=wave function=mathematical description of the wave)

Born once again came up with an ingenious idea for the interpretation of the wave—just like he had in the case of Heisenberg. He opined that the square of the wave function (the wave function is one of the solutions of the Schrödinger Equation) indicates a probability. This probability does not describe a particle of matter as such, but the probability of finding it in a certain location. Hence, the wave is a probability wave that is not actually real. It does not exist in the world we know, but in a mysterious spirit world. The entire subject matter is a tad mystical and increasingly headed in the direction of metaphysics, which is also the reason why, over the course of their lives, Heisenberg and Schrödinger dwelled increasingly on questions arising from this field, as well as various religions and philosophy.

Schrödinger also won acclaim outside of the field of physics when he proposed a thought experiment called *Schrödinger's Cat*. It investigates the possible consequences of transferring the terms of quantum physics to our everyday world and leads to the insane paradox that a cat can be simultaneously dead and alive. The Coen Brothers devised this topic impressively in their movie *"A Serious Man."* An individual who has both, the characteristics of a dead body and a person who is alive, appears in the introductory story. The film *"Inside Llewyn Davis"* also makes references to the dead cat and the cat that is alive. For those who are fans of the TV series *"Big Bang Theory,"* I recommend you watch the episode in which attempts to resolve a relationship problem with the assistance of Schrödinger's thought experiment are made (see e.g. http://www.youtube.com/watch?v=HCOE__N6v4o).

Quantum mechanics, as formulated mathematically by Schrödinger and Heisenberg, have made an incredible conquest and still have few rivals. Along with the theory of relativity, this discipline can safely be called the most spectacular and successful physics theory of all times. To date, it has never been contradicted and it has never failed.

All of the founding fathers of quantum physics, i.e. Planck, Einstein, Bohr, Heisenberg, Pauli, Schrödinger, Dirac and Born were awarded Nobel Prizes in Physics for their discoveries. Curiously, Albert Einstein did not receive a Nobel Prize for his theory of relativity, but for the description of a quantum effect. His scientific work on the so-called photoelectric effect remains the physical foundation for solar cells even as we speak.

Einstein later emerged as a bitter opponent of quantum physics because he was unable to accept this discipline's philosophical consequences. He kept coming up with new thought experiments in order to contradict the new physics, but remained unsuccessful in his attempts until the day of his death. Time and again, quantum physics turned out to be correct.

The theory of quantum physics dominates our everyday lives, although most of us don't have a clue that it does. The electronic alarm clocks that wakes you up in the morning is quantum effects based, just like the PC you may be working on right now. If you go shopping after work and the cashier scans in your purchases during the check-out process, you are experiencing another effect of quantum physics. Or maybe you had an MRI (magnetic resonance imaging) examination at your doctor's office. You guessed it, the functions of this medical device also hinge on computations performed with the assistance of quantum mechanics. Do you know the sources of your electrical power? Does it come from nuclear power plants or solar cells? The two are indeed two completely different technologies, but they are both based on the effects of quantum physics.

According to Prof. Harald Lesch, an astrophysicist at the University of Munich, about 40 % of all of the world's gross domestic products combined is based on the fundamentals of quantum theory. Nonetheless, the interpretation of quantum theory is still shrouded in mystery today and remains unsolved - more than 100 years after its discovery. Now this book aims to make a new attempt to solve it.

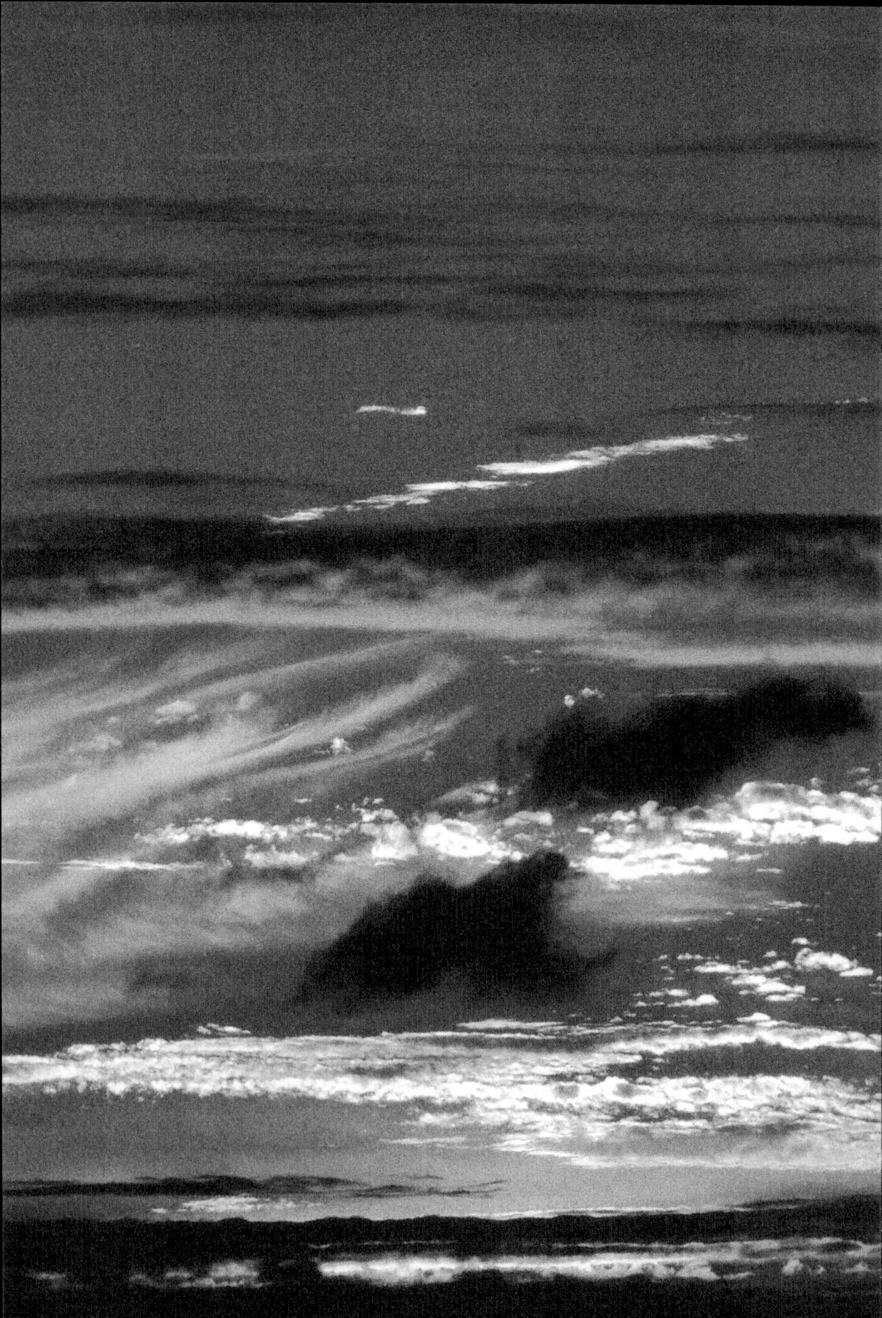

3. How to alter the course of the past

It was 6 in the morning on a day in April in 1905. The young man, just 26 years of age, had come to work early that day. He was glad to have landed the job at the patent office in Bern, Switzerland. After all, he had a wife and a son to take care of. The family shared a two bedroom apartment at the time. Just like every day from Monday to Saturday, he had walked to work from home. In his hand he had a document consisting of just a few pages, which he was going to send to the German Physics Magazine that same day.

This scientific work was bound to turn Newton's physical theory, which had been the scientific law to live by for centuries and had been devised by the most admired genius in the history of science, on its head. The young man's treatise focused on the essence of time. His conclusions contradict common sense to such an extent that even today many people find it difficult to believe them to be true. The name of the young man: Albert Einstein. His "special theory of relativity" was later revealed to a large majority of the population under this name, although only very few actually understood it. A few years after his work was first published virtually every child was familiar with the name Albert Einstein. Besides Charlie Chaplin, he was one of the first great worldwide superstars.

In 1905, Einstein had not only published his description of the theory of relativity, but had also made another discovery in the field of quantum physics. The discovery that it is possible to explain the phenomenon of light based on waves dates back as far as the 17th century. After all, it is very similar to the waves that occur in water. Einstein's discovery focused on the question of how one could describe the photoelectric effect differently because waves could not be used for this purpose. One of the ideas was to use particles that have different behavior patterns than waves.

In this context, let's have a look at the structure of the experiment shown in Figure 1.

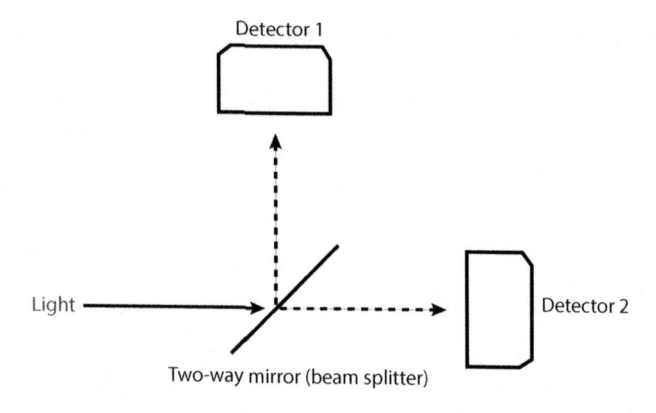

Figure 1: Light behaving like a particle

From the left, light falls on a two-way mirror (beam splitter), which directs some of the light towards the top towards detector 1, where it is registered. The remaining light is simply allowed to penetrate through the mirror and reaches detector 2.

You may be familiar with two-way from watching certain detective series on TV. They frequently feature interrogation scenes and also line-ups. Witnesses are asked to come to the precinct to possibly identify a suspect. They are taken into a room that is separated from another room by a two-way mirror. The detectives and the witness are in the darkened room on one side, while the lined up potential suspects are standing in a row in the other, brightly lit room. In this situation, the witness can see the suspects, but they cannot see anyone in the other room.

But I digress; let's get back to our experiment. Let's presume light actually consisted of particles (photons). One photon comes into contact with the two-way mirror. It ensures that it either passes through to detector 2 or reflected to detector 1. Logic tells us that this is an "either or" decision. Of course you are also familiar with such finite questions in your everyday life: people are either married or single. An interim state does not exist. It's the same way with our photon. It will never be simultaneously present in both directions. It either passes through the mirror or the mirror redirects it to the top.

Things would be different if the light was a wave. If it were, it would be possible to measure it on both detectors at all times, because a wave is expansive and can travel on multiple paths simultaneously. For instance, if a wave moves forward in a river and encounters a fork, it will split up and travel on both channels at the same time. Consequently, waves are not separate objects, but expand across wider spaces. Hence, they are also not indivisible while elementary particles such as the photons are.

In other words, the experiment is a test that determines whether light consists of waves or particles. If at a certain point in time only detector 1 or detector 2 receives a signal, light is composed of individual particles. However, if both detectors indicate action simultaneously, the light is composed of waves. That's the experiment we are conducting here.

So—what is the result of our experiment? Scientists determined that the light can be seen only on one detector at a time; never simultaneously on both. Hence, the light consists of photons. So far, so good. Actually we could now conclude this Chapter based on this discovery—if it were not for the fact that yet another experiment has been conducted.

The same set-up is also used for this experiment. Light falls on a beam splitter and is once again either allowed to pass through or is diverted. However, detector 1 is replaced with a normal mirror that reflects the light in the direction of detector 2. We also replace detector 2 with film that will register the light. Our test set-up looks like this:

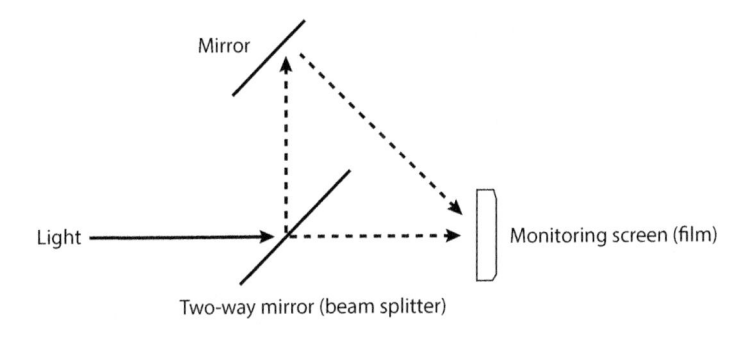

Figure 2: Light behaving like a wave

So what happens this time? At the beginning of the experiment, the light photons collide with different areas of the monitoring screen (film). However, after some time, something surprising happens. A pattern consisting of bright and dark stripes appears on the screen. What created this pattern? One of the typical things waves do when they collide is form a pattern. Cast two rocks into the water at the same time and you will see them creating waves that expand in all directions. As a result, an interesting pattern of overlapping waves develops. In physics the term for these patterns is "interference." If two wave crests or two wave troughs collide, they add together constructively. Crests become higher and troughs become deeper. However, if a wave crest and a wave trough collide, they neutralize each other as if a wave had never even existed (destructive interference). We are also familiar with the effects of wave crest overlaps and their devastating consequences because we have observed them in natural disasters. During a tsunami, many small wave crests initially begin to overlap near the beach until they consolidate into high, destructive monster waves (constructive interference).

The result of the experiment is definitive: light acts like a wave that is split into two partial waves when it comes into contact with the two-way mirror, which in turn strike the film. A striped interference pattern is created on the surface of the film. This is similar to what happens with the two rocks that are flung into the water.

The physicists had to wait until 1986 when French physicist Alain Aspect and his team were able to complete the above-described experiment successfully. Although the wave nature of light had been established as a fact quite some time ago, it was Alain Aspect who was able to measure light in the form of a wave and of a photon by making just a minor change to the experiment's set-up.

So what is light—a wave or a particle? It appears as if the answer to this question hinges on the set-up of the experiment. If we check the path the light has taken, it acts like a particle. That's the outcome of the experiment described in Figure 1. However, if our objective is not to verify the path of the light, it takes on the characteristics of waves. Figure 2 illustrates this experiment.

Contrary to human intuition and our everyday experiences, light is not part of an objective world that exists autonomously from our observations. This may sound rather crazy, but can be clearly verified in experiments. As far as light is concerned, we find ourselves confronted with schizophrenic behavior patterns—patterns that are typical for quantum objects. Particle and wave—light is both—depending how it is measured and how you set up an experiment.

The mysterious light

Let's assume the role of light for an instance. At the beginning of the experiment it encounters the beam splitter (Figure 1). "I see," it thinks, "The person conducting the experiment wants to know which path I will take. So, I'll quickly convert myself into a particle as soon as I reach the beam splitter."

Next, we modify the set-up of the experiment and replace the two detectors with a mirror and a piece of film (Figure 2). The light's response: "You can't fool me, I can see right away that the experiment has been changed." So the light quickly assumes the role of a wave.

John Wheeler, a physicist from the United States, came up with an experiment that would trick the light. He referred to his concept as the "Delayed Choice Experiment". Numerous universities and research institutions have already conducted it successfully.

Here is how this experiment works: light encounters the beam splitter and sees the test set-up depicted in Figure 1. The photon is diverted at the beam splitter and is en route to Detector 1. However, the distance between the beam splitter and the detector is so gigantic this time that it takes the light quite some time to cover the distance. At the very last moment—just before the photon encounters Detector 1—we replace Detector 1 with the mirror and Detector 2 with a film. As a consequence, we are modifying the entire set-up of the experiment while the light is still traveling. Hence, our version of the experiment is the one shown in Figure 2, in which we have measured light as a wave. In reality, the scientists are indeed working very quickly, but not fast enough to replace the two detectors with the mirror and the film. That's why special electrical switches are used for this experiment as well as a so-called Mach-Zehnder interferometer; however, principally, this is the same type of experimental set-up as the one used in our example.

So what is the result of this experiment? We actually find interference patterns that are typical for waves in the location where Detector 2 has been replaced with film. If we had not replaced the two detectors with the mirror and film, we would have obtained a result typically produced by individual particles.

The result is confusing. After all, we were under the impression that the light, once it has encountered the beam splitter and leaves it, is already a wave or a particle. However, we obviously do not determine whether the light we have obtained is a wave or a particle until we conduct measurements (make an observation).

Upon closer examination, the result is even more perplexing. Wheeler concluded that:

"by making a delayed decision, we inevitably affect what we are permitted to say rightfully about the past history of the photon."

To put it into more drastic terms: we actually changed the past of the light retroactively! Something, that is not possible in the normal everyday world we live in to date, happens readily in the world of light quanta. Unfortunately, it is not possible to accommodate the desire of so many people to reverse their own pasts and wrong decisions they have made. Apparently, things are different in the world of light.

In physics, the above-described light phenomenon is referred to as a non-locality in time. This means that it is no longer possible to distinguish between the past, present and future. In this state, time-based distances (gaps in time or time intervals) do not exist any longer. Our everyday lives have taught us to believe that we do not have any control over the past, but that we can affect our future by the actions we take in the present. In other words, our access to the past differs from the access we have to the future. If our regular everyday world were non-local from a timing perspective, our access to the future would be similar to the access we have to the past. The phenomenon determined through our experiment may cause many to liken it to the theological term "eternity." It certainly occurred to me. Is this only a passing notion or does it have an actual, much deeper, meaning? And if so, is light in a state of eternity? We will examine these questions more thoroughly in Chapter 4.

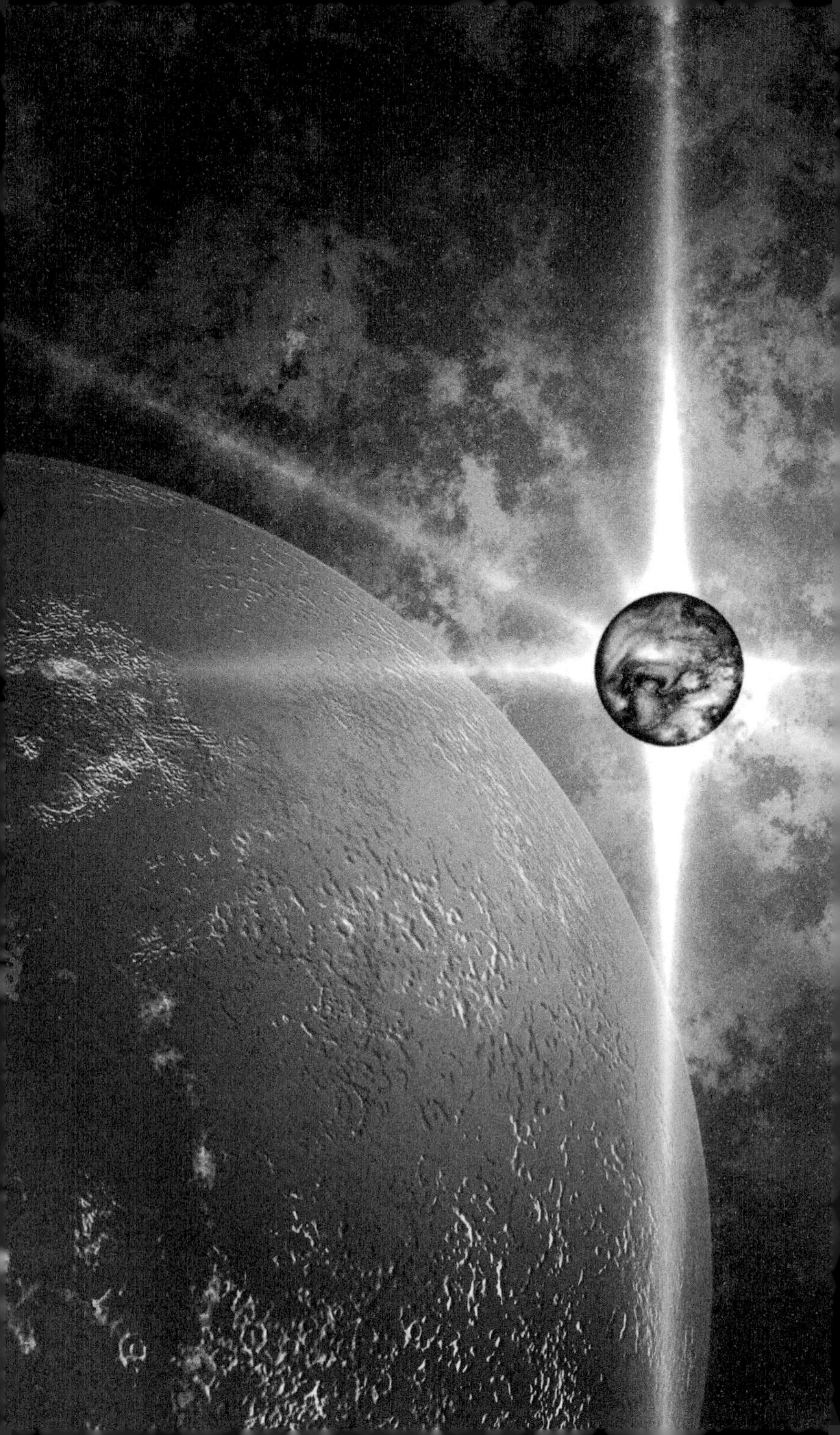

4. What does "eternity" mean?

To be able to enjoy the peace and quiet I needed to write my book, I sought refuge at the Lichtenthal Monastery in Baden-Baden (a town in the southwestern part of Germany) for a few days during Holy Week. Alongside the small Oos River I had intoxicating views of the magnificent colors of the magnolias, which had just begun to bloom. I was on my way back to the monastery from an earlier tour of the William Copley art exhibit at the Burda Museum when I spotted two paragliders above me up in the air. While the Merkur, the point of departure for the gliders and Baden-Baden's own mountain is easily visible from the monastery, I had never before seen paragliders who got this close to downtown Baden-Baden. I instantly wondered how they contemplated the city from way above, gliding silently through the air? Where would they land? Just a moment later, they both gently set down on the vast meadow adjacent to the monastery.

What is the purpose of time?
The Delayed Choice experiment we talked about in Chapter 3 demonstrated that light does turn our standard ideas of the characteristics of time on its head. Normally, we divide time into past, present and future. From our everyday lives we all know that the past is over and done with and that it never returns. We can't revise it; all we can do is remember it. This is especially true for the emotional events in our lives—regardless of whether they were negative or positive experiences. Most of us probably remember where we were the day the airplanes crashed into the World Trade Center or the first time we exchanged kisses with our partners. The future, on the other hand, holds things in store for us—things that have not happened yet; the future is ahead of us. We often attempt to foresee future events or to plan ahead of time and aren't always successful. The present tense is hard to grasp. It, however, is the real time—the time during which events occur.

Let's go back to my story about the paragliders. When they took off from the Merkur, their departure time—the exact time they lifted off—was the present—at that very moment. From the paragliders' perspective, they would land in both, the here and now as well as in the future. There is a time gap (time interval) between both of these incidents—a gap that separates the present tense from a certain point in time in the future.

One could also say that it separates reality from the possible. After all, the moment they took off was real for them at the time. They did not know precisely where they would eventually land. Would the thermal effects carry them to the foot of the mountain near the Valley Station or all the way down to the meadow by the monastery? Those were the potential landing places.

Gaps in time do make sequences possible. These step-by-step sequences are what it takes for us to be able to develop, learn things and acquire new experiences; such as the flight of the paragliders from the Merkur down to the meadow by the monastery. Now try to remember how you learned to speak, for instance, a new language or to play, a musical instrument or a new athletic discipline. It always took time periods—or gaps in time.

What is eternity?

Time gaps between past, present and future no longer exist in the light quantum experiment discussed in Chapter 3. We referred to this state as non-locality in time. Is this term also related to the term "eternity" we are familiar with from theology? What pops into your mind spontaneously if you hear the word "eternity?" Do you envision and infinitely long, never-ending time frame or timelessness? Or something completely different? Many theologians tend to argue in favor of timelessness. Interestingly enough, there are also those who define eternity the same way they define the characteristics of light we have learned about in Chapter 3. Actually, they may do this without even being aware of it. One of the theologians who define eternity the same way it is defined in quantum physics, is Joseph Ratzinger—the former Pope –, who penned the book *Einführung in das Christentum (An Introduction to Christianity)* while he was a professor at the University of Tübingen. Let's examine his conclusion on the subject matter of eternity more closely:

> *"It (eternity) is not timelessness, but time power. Taking on the role of today, which is equivalent to all tenses, it can also have a continued impact on any time."*

This line gives us the keywords that are relevant to eternity: not timelessness, but time power, equivalent to all tenses and with an effect on all times. Obviously, the quanta of light are in a state of eternity if we apply Joseph Ratzinger's definitions to them. After all, the light has the power to have an effect on the past and to retroactively transform itself into a wave or a photon. In the present moment, all tenses are the same for the light—there are no time gaps between the past, the present and the future.

However, the conclusions described above were not only made by theologians of our day and age, but date back several centuries. For instance, Christian mystic Meister Eckhart did express very similar thoughts, as evident from the definition of eternity on the German Wikipedia page, which translates into this statement:

"The now in which God made the first man and the now in which the last man on earth will perish and the now in which I am speaking to you—they're all the same and they are nothing but a now. . . . which is why what is inherent in him (the human being living in the present) is neither suffering nor sequence of time, but consistent eternity."

If, according to Meister Eckhart, time sequences do not exist, we are physically in a state of non-locality in time, i.e. in a state in which all time gaps disappear.

We can draw an astounding conclusion from what has been said so far. Given that the light behaves in a non-local state in time, it is in a state of eternity. Eternity does not mean timelessness or an infinite amount of time, but states that all times occur simultaneously in the present moment.

The light and eternity

In the eyes of Christians, light has a unique meaning and is often used as a symbol for God.

For instance, the Book of John I 1.5 states:

"This is the message we have heard from him and proclaim to you, that God is light and in him there is no darkness at all. . . ."

Many theological books assign eternity to God as one of His characteristics. Hence, we can view light as a symbol for God who is in a state of eternity—the simultaneous existence in the past, present and future in the present moment.

If you elaborate on this thought and think it through, you will be able to devise an even more amazing conclusion: eternity does not begin in the afterlife, but in this life down here on earth. Hence, it is definitely present and possible anytime during our lifetime.

You may not be very comfortable with this thought and it might even sound strange. If so, you are experiencing what I felt when I first became aware of the relationship and links between modern quantum physics and theology. The similarities between the teachings of Jesus Christ and those of quantum physics are surprising. The statement "nor will people say, 'Here it is,' or 'There it is,' because the kingdom of God is in your midst." (Luke 17, 21) points out that the Kingdom of God begins here in our lifetime on earth, not just in Heaven after we have passed. This is comparable to the quantum physics teaching that eternity—a characteristic of God—is already present in our midst. As you continue reading this book, you will find other statements Jesus made, which are congruent with the teachings of modern quantum physics. That's why the title of this book is—Jesus Christ—Quantum Physicist.

So far, we have familiarized ourselves with the phenomenon of non-locality in time. In the next Chapter we will look into non-locality in space, to subsequently ask ourselves whether there are also parallels to the omnipresence of God

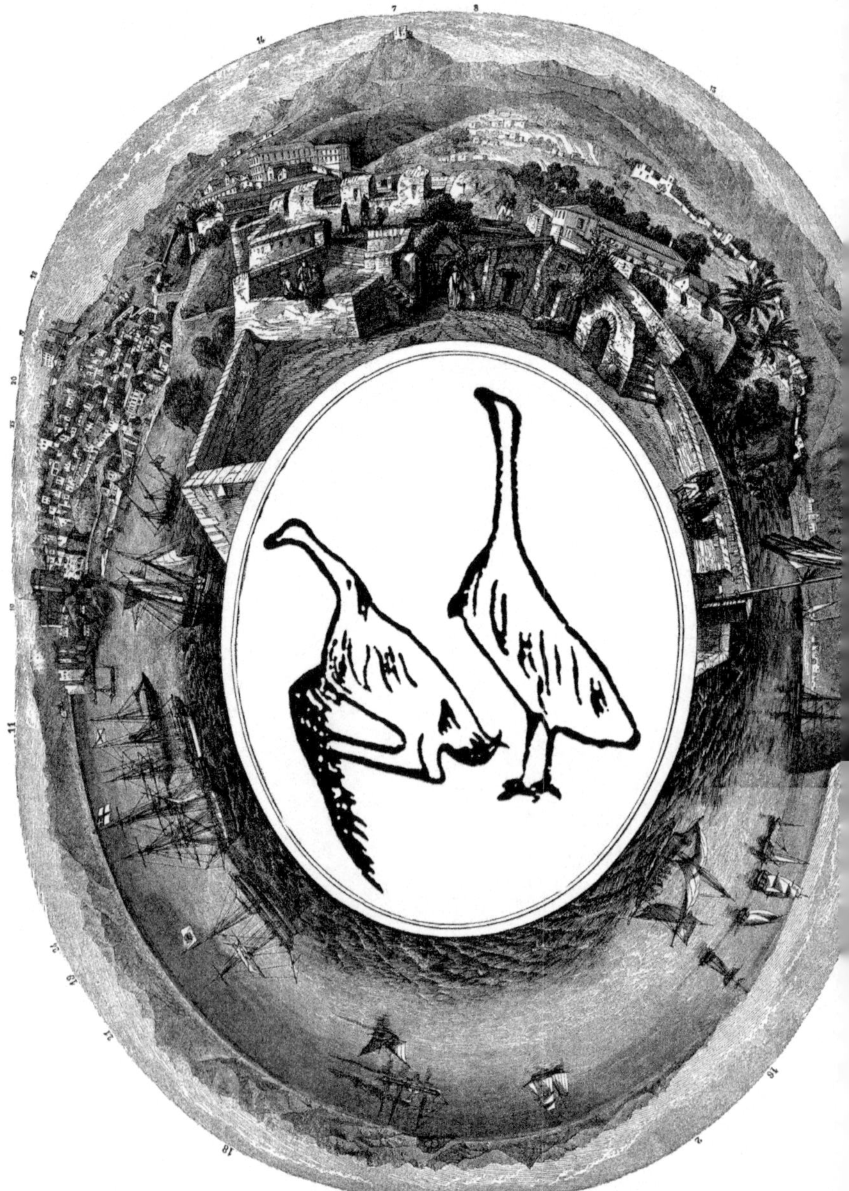

5. Why New York is a neighboring city of San Francisco

As a thought experiment, imagine a cosmic catastrophe—one where the sun disappears completely in a mere second. When would we earthlings realize that the sun is gone? Would its light be gone in a moment so that the day would instantly turn into night? Amazingly, this would only happen about eight and a half minutes after the cosmic disaster. This is how much time it takes the light to reach the earth from the sun. For these eight and a half minutes, nobody on earth would be aware of the disaster; not even the scientists and their measuring devices. However, anyone who is in close proximity to the sun would almost instantly know that the sun has disappeared.

In physics, such scenarios are called locality in space (geographic locality). This term means that whatever happens there and now does initially not affect what is happening here and now. Initially, changes affect only their immediate proximity—i.e. they have local effects. You are familiar with this because it is evident in some local weather scenarios. While it's raining in Saint Paul, the sun may shine just across the river in Minneapolis.

The opposite of locality in space (geographic locality) is non-locality in space. In the latter scenario, events would have an immediate effect everywhere—an effect that is of random vastness and may even extend to the entire universe. Prior to the discovery of quantum physics, natural scientists were familiar with local theories only.

In 1935, the previously mentioned Erwin Schrödinger was the first to introduce the term "entanglement" into quantum physics. What does this term mean? Let's use a thought experiment to examine this further. Two individuals—we'll call them Bob and Alice—one lives in San Francisco and the other in New York, are both dropping a coin on the ground at the exact same time. Each coin has two possible symbols that face up after they've been dropped—a number or a coat of arms. These states were not pre-defined. However, in our special scenario, these are not just common coins, but quantum coins, which create the following scenarios: whenever Bob gets a number facing up, Alice gets a coat of arms and vice-versa. They never get a number or coat of arms at the same time. The two coins are mysteriously connected with each other over vast distances. They are always entangled.

Of course such coins do not exist in the everyday world we live in. Nevertheless, such scenarios ARE possible in the quantum world. So what are the prerequisites for the existence of such entanglements? One capability the two coins have to have for such an entanglement to come to fruition is that they can tell each other on what side they have just landed. Imagine the coins had brains and were able to communicate with each other. Hence, the coin in San Francisco (Bob) would have the ability to send a text message to the coin in New York (Alice): "Landed on coat of arms. You have to land on the number. Bob." Let's also presume the events have to be accurate down to one hundredth of a second—just like in a 100-meter-sprint in track and fields. We'd have a huge problem if this were the case. Given that San Francisco and New York are such a vast distance apart, the transmission of the information even at the speed of light would take more than a hundredth of a second. This means that the signal would have to travel faster than light. However, according to Albert Einstein's theory of relativity, speeds that are faster than the speed of light are prohibited. Consequently, such phenomena cannot exist in our everyday world. In it, all we have are the previously mentioned local theories that state that it always takes a certain amount of time until signals are transmitted through space.

What about the world of quantum physics? In 1951, U.S. physicist David Bohm came up with an experiment that examines the behavior of two quantum objects. He suggested the measurement of the spin. The objects may be particles such as electrons, for instance. To explain it visually, a spinning particle acts like a gyroscope that turns in a certain direction; similar to a roundabout that can move counter-clockwise and clockwise. Unfortunately, this comparison of the mysterious world of quantum physics with an example from our everyday lives is somewhat problematic since the particles only pretend to be turning. They don't actually turn. However, to make the spin easier to visualize, let's use this example.

At the start of the experiment, the two quantum particles have to be prepared in such a manner that they turn in opposite directions. Physicists also say that the total spin of both of these particles is equivalent to zero. What's important is that the total spin of such a system cannot change due to the conservation laws of physics. When conducting a measurement, a right turn is measured, for instance, on an electron. At the same time, given the triggered conservation law, a left turn is automatically determined on the other electron. So, looking back at the previous Chapters, remember that the characteristics of a quantum object are not determined before monitoring (measuring) it. In the case of the light quantum, we did not determine whether the light appears as a particle or a wave until we chose the type of measurement. A similar scenario applies to our turning electrons. We determine the rotation direction through our measurement. Before we perform the measurement we are not in a position to say which electron is moving counter-clockwise. We only know that both electrons rotate in opposite directions at the precise moment we observe them.

Alain Aspect—the physicist we referred to earlier—and his team conducted quantum photon entanglement experiments as far back as 1982. To test the Theorem, Aspect and his team sent photons flying in opposite directions and conducted so-called polarization measurements on them. To visualize this, polarization is the vibration direction of light (up and down or side to side, vibrations or any other angle). Similar to the earlier described spin measurements, the direction of the polarization is not determined until concrete measurements are taken of the photons. The results are baffling. If one determines the polarization of one photon by observing it, the polarization of the other photon is automatically and instantly caused by that observation, regardless of how far apart the photons might be. How is this possible? In order to be able to explain the experiments, the information concerning the polarization of one photon would have to be transmitted to the other photon via space at a speed that is faster than the speed of light. However, in a local world, this is impossible based on Albert Einstein's theory of relativity.

Getting back to our coin throwing experiment, this would mean that there is virtually no distance between San Francisco and New York, i.e. that both cities are in the same location. It would be great if this were also possible in our conventional world as we would no longer have to spend hours as weary travelers en route to far away destinations.

In Chapters 3 and 4, we familiarized ourselves with non-locality in time, which erases the gaps between past, present and future. In the current scenario, we have a similar effect, albeit this one is space related. Consequently, the phenomenon is called non-locality in space. It describes a state in which there is no geographic distance between the objects.

So, does this mean that quantum physics is a geographic non-local theory or can the result of Aspect's experiments also be justified on the grounds of a local theory? There is, in fact, another explanation that could use a local theory as a justification. It's a local theory with so-called hidden variables. One classic example would be the following situation: an apple is cut into two halves and placed into the soil in two different fields that are located at a great distance from each other. After some time, one can determine that the apple trees that grow from the seeds have similar properties, such as the same shape of leaves. How is this possible in the absence of any communication between the two plants? The explanation: genetics. After all, the genes of the plant predetermine certain characteristics of the tree. If researchers were not aware of the theory of genetics, this would be a hidden variable. Such hidden variables might also exist in our experiment of entangled electrons. This means that the properties might be predetermined and that the scientists are not aware of it.

It was a groundbreaking stroke of genius when Irish physicist John Bell came up with the Bell's Theorem, which was obviously named for him, in 1965. He had devised an experiment that clarifies whether hidden parameters can be used to explain quantum physics. Bell derived a mathematical inequality from certain assumptions, which focuses on the logical rules all measuring processes are subject to.

One perfect example of Bell's Theorem would be census taking. These counts will likely not produce results claiming that there are more blonde Americans than there are blonde men in the United States and blonde women of all nationalities in the world combined (including all blonde women in the United States). The result of the experiment proposed by Bell and based on polarization of photons is astounding. It is not possible to explain the non-locality in space with the assistance of hidden variables.

Reality is transcendent
So what does all of this mean for us? In a geographically non-local world (non-locality in space) something may happen at the one end of the universe and may have an instant impact on us. The distance is completely irrelevant. On the other hand, it is of course also possible that an experiment we perform in the here and now has an instant impact on a

system that is far away. According to Einstein, such momentary effects across vast distances are not permitted because they would have to spread at a speed higher than the speed of light, which is prohibited according to his special theory of relativity. Consequently, Einstein called this effect "spooky action at a distance" and tried to refute it through thought experiments for the rest of his life—unsuccessfully. Quantum physics always proved to be correct.

At first, the consequences of non-locality in space sound rather harmless. However, some scientists who have done comprehensive non-locality related work have arrived at astounding conclusions. In his book *Versteckte Wirklichkeit (Hidden Reality)*, physicist Prof. Lothar Schäfer, who taught at the University of Arkansas, examines this topic with great intensity. For instance, he mentions physicists D'Espagnat and Aspect, who devised well-founded arguments supporting the theory that non-locality is not only a phenomenon that arises in experiments under precisely defined conditions, but also a characteristic of reality as such. In other words, a characteristic we encounter in our everyday lives.

Physicists Stapp, Kafatos, Nadeau, Goswami and Nesteruk took this theory even further. Corroborated by experiments, the fact that quantum objects behave as if geographic distance doesn't exist, forces them to conclude that tangible objects are interconnected beyond our perceivable universe. They make this claim although, in our everyday world and based on our experience, objects are clearly separated from each other.

Based on the above, the authors arrive at the conclusion that non-locality in space indicates that there is a transcendence. It appears as if something, that can be described as transcendent, exists that does affect our world.

So what does transcendence mean? It would be incorrect to imagine that the transcendent realm is another box that frames our universe. In my opinion, the previously mentioned physicist, Lothar Schäfer, already found the proper definition for this term in his book *Versteckte Wirklichkeit (Hidden Reality)*, a translation of which can be found below:
"I refer to all aspects, elements or conditions of our existence that are beyond our direct control, beyond the visible surface of objects and beyond any justification we can come up with through our intellect and sensual

> *experience as transcendent. Transcendent reality, for instance, is a component of physical reality that we cannot observe directly."*

All of this would have a dramatic impact on our worldview. Processes beyond our universe exist in a transcendent range and affect the things that happen in our world. This is a vision many people find hard to accept.

So, let's sum it up: quantum objects behave as if time and space do not exist. They act as if there are in fact no geographic and time-based distances. They are present everywhere in space—unfettered from time—eternal.

In Chapter 4, we have already established a connection between theology and quantum physics by linking time-based non-locality with eternity. To that end, we have determined that time gaps between past, present and future do not exist. Hence, in the context of geographic non-locality, it makes sense to wonder whether the omnipresence of God could have something to do with the non-locality in space in quantum physics. We will examine this further in Chapter 6.

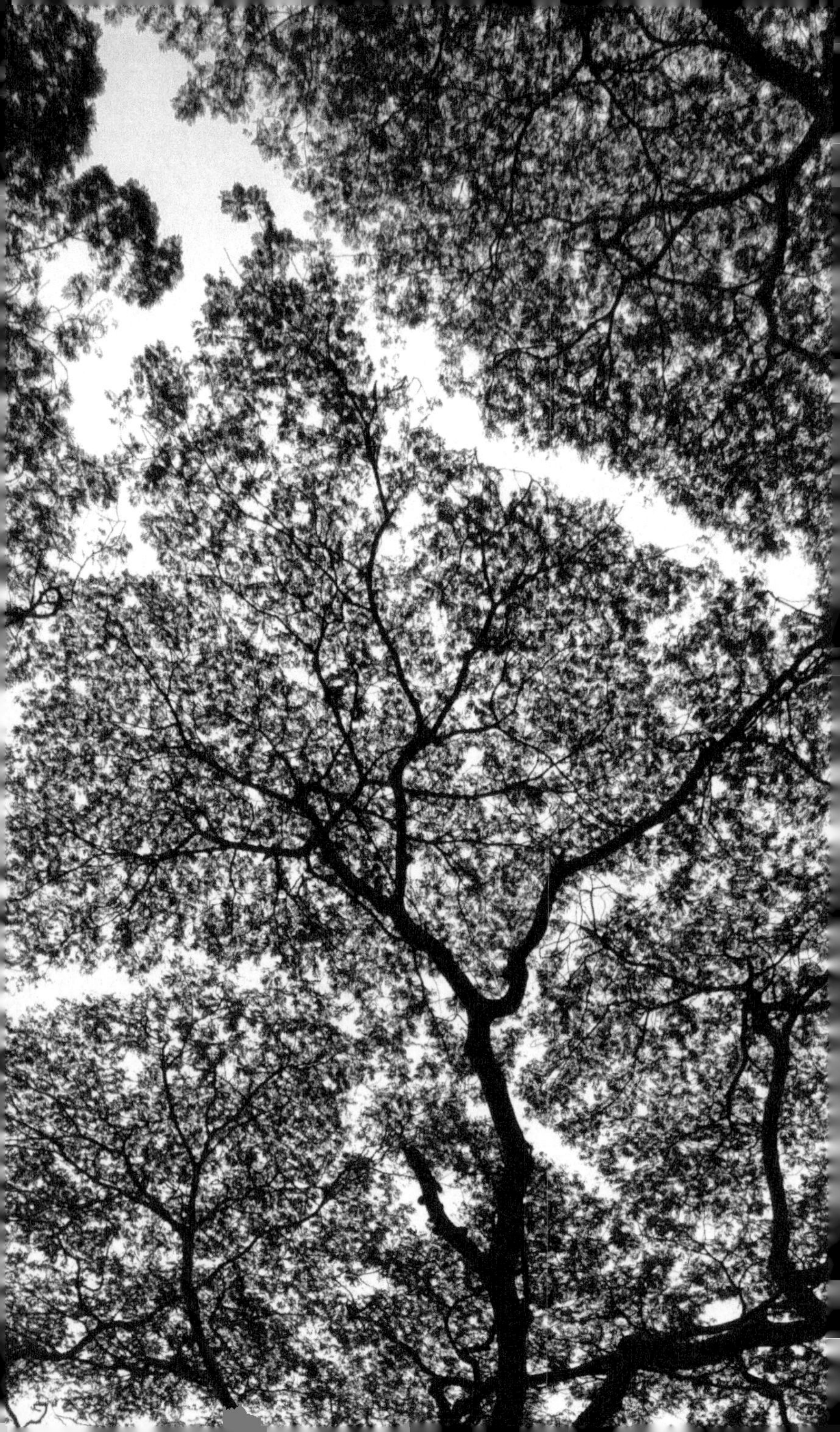

6. What is omnipresence?

In our everyday lives, we are accustomed to linking the characteristics of an object to its location. When we cynically say "That matters just about as much to me as if I had just learned that a bag of rice fell over in China today," what we are trying to express is that something is completely irrelevant and useless information for us because it concerns something minor that happened in a far-away place. When you take this stance vis-à-vis natural science, it has a similar meaning. In this case, it refers to action that occurs at a remote location and does not have any impact on the things that are going on in my present location—i.e. local action.

The experiment described in the previous Chapter shows us a completely different phenomenon. The performance of a measurement on an electron results in a second electron in a place far from the first one being instantly impacted. This happens as if there were no distance between them at all. At least this is the case if both of these particles are entangled with each other.

Theology defines God as a being that sublimely rules over space and time. Terms such as omnipresence and eternity are used to describe his level of freedom. However, what does the omnipresence of God mean? Many of us imagine God to be present anywhere in our universe.

Let's check what the Bible tells us about the omnipresence of God:

Psalm 139.7:
"Where can I go from your spirit? Or where can I flee from your presence? If I ascend to heaven, you are there; if I make my bed in Sheol, you are there. If I take the wings of the morning and settle at the farthest limits of the sea, even there your hand shall lead me, and your right hand shall hold me fast."

Hence, based on Scripture, God is present everywhere—throughout the world—simultaneously.

How could one even imagine the possibility of being in all places of the world at the same time? Let's just say, if you find yourself standing on the skyline platform of the Empire States Building, enjoying the magnificent views, you are in Manhattan, New York at the time. While you are there, you no longer have a geographic distance from the Empire State Building—after all, you are right on location.

Nonetheless, at the same moment, you are within a geographic distance from all other U.S. metropolises. For instance, from where you are, you'd have to travel more than a thousand miles to get to San Francisco or Dallas. Given the geographic distance, it would be impossible for you to be in both of these other places at the same time.

Again, things are different in the quantum world with its non-locality. In it, distances between two particles that are entangled with each other obviously do not exist any longer. This means that in a place of non-locality in space, you would have the ability to be in all places at the same time because distances do not exist. This, of course, is the very definition the Bible uses to describe God's omnipresence—He is simultaneously present in all locations.

Consequently, we can identify a congruent thought in both theology and natural science as soon as we view non-locality in space the same way we interpret the omnipresence of God.

In his book *Lucy im Licht (Lucy in the Light)*, Markolf Niemz, a physics professor who conducts research at the University of Heidelberg (Germany), makes the presumption that entangled particles or photons are actually not two particles.

"This is why I believe that all of the observations made to justify the term "entanglement" can also be explained differently; specifically—and this is the key criterion—in a much simpler way. Why simpler? Because the entangled particles, in my opinion, do not only act as if they were a single object, but in fact comprise only a single object. In other words: Because they simply aren't different particles, but merely represent different aspects of one whole unit."

Markolf Niemz's thoughts, for which he provides scientific justifications in his book, are surprisingly identical with a statement made in Romans, 11.36:
"For of him, and through him, and to him, are all things: to whom be glory for ever." or *"I and the Father are one"* (John 10:30).

The world is seen as a whole entity. The quote from the Bible points into the same direction as Markolf Niemz's conclusion on the entanglement phenomenon. Based on this interpretation, all tangible objects would actually not be separated at all, but would have their roots in a transcendent and godly primordial source. On God's level, all objects and sentient beings in this world would be one entity.

These considerations are corroborated by the conclusions we arrived at in Chapter 5 in references to transcendence. Specifically the concept that tangible objects are interconnected beyond the reach of our space and time (physicists call it space-time), i.e. in a transcendental spectrum, although they appear to be geographically separated in our universe.

Another interesting observation in this context is that the sphere Jesus defines as the Kingdom of God does have the same characteristics as the geographic non-locality and therefore the omnipresence of God.

> Luke 17.20–21:
> "Once Jesus was asked by the Pharisees when the kingdom of God was coming, and he answered, 'The kingdom of God is not coming with things that can be observed; nor will they say, "Look, here it is!" or "There it is!" For, in fact, the kingdom of God is among you."

Just like it would not make sense to talk about a specific location and therefore a here and there when making reference to the Kingdom of God as Jesus describes it, this would be completely out of place when describing entangled particles, given that geographic distances do not even exist between these objects any longer. Jesus' elaboration (Luke 17.20–21) on the Kingdom of God surprisingly also reveals, that this Kingdom already exists during our lifetime and that it is forever present in our midst. In other words, we do not have to wait for it until after we pass on, as so many of us believe. Yet it is difficult to recognize this fact since these characteristics are not ours to observe in our common everyday world. This is congruent with the claims made in modern quantum physics, which have determined the existence of non-locality in space and in time in the here and now. However, this discovery has only been made among the tiniest quantum objects of the microcosm—comprising atoms and elementary particles. In our everyday lives we nonetheless only interact with objects such as chairs, tables, cups and other items that are located in certain areas of the room or space at a specific point and time. Geographic distances and time gaps do exist as far as these objects are concerned, although they are, in fact, whole units composed of these tiny quantum objects.

Why is there a need for space or room?

At this point you may wonder why there even is a need for geographic distances. Remember the paragliders scenario I described in Chapter 4? From my perspective, the paragliders were up in the air while I was down on the ground. However, from the paragliders' point of view, the situation was completely different: they were in the air and I was down on the ground. In other words, geography separates the there from the here. There's some space between us. Hence, the paragliders have some leeway they can utilize; for instance, to land in the meadow. But the paragliders can also use this space to do other things, as long as they do not encroach upon the personal freedom of another human or sentient being. Geographic distance also allows us to be on the other side and makes individuality possible. In the absence of geographic distance—and this is truly important—it is not possible to establish relationships, neither with other people nor with God. After all, to be able to enter into a relationship, there has to be space between the individuals so that they can experience feelings of closeness, but also the freedom of distance.

Non-locality in space and time allows us to arrive at the following conclusion: Given that geographic and time-based distances do not exist for quantum objects, they are in a state of eternity and omnipresence because all times and places can be perceived at the same time. In theology, these two characteristics are attributes of God. So is the quantum world a parable for God? To examine this question more thoroughly, we will first look at a riveting experiment.

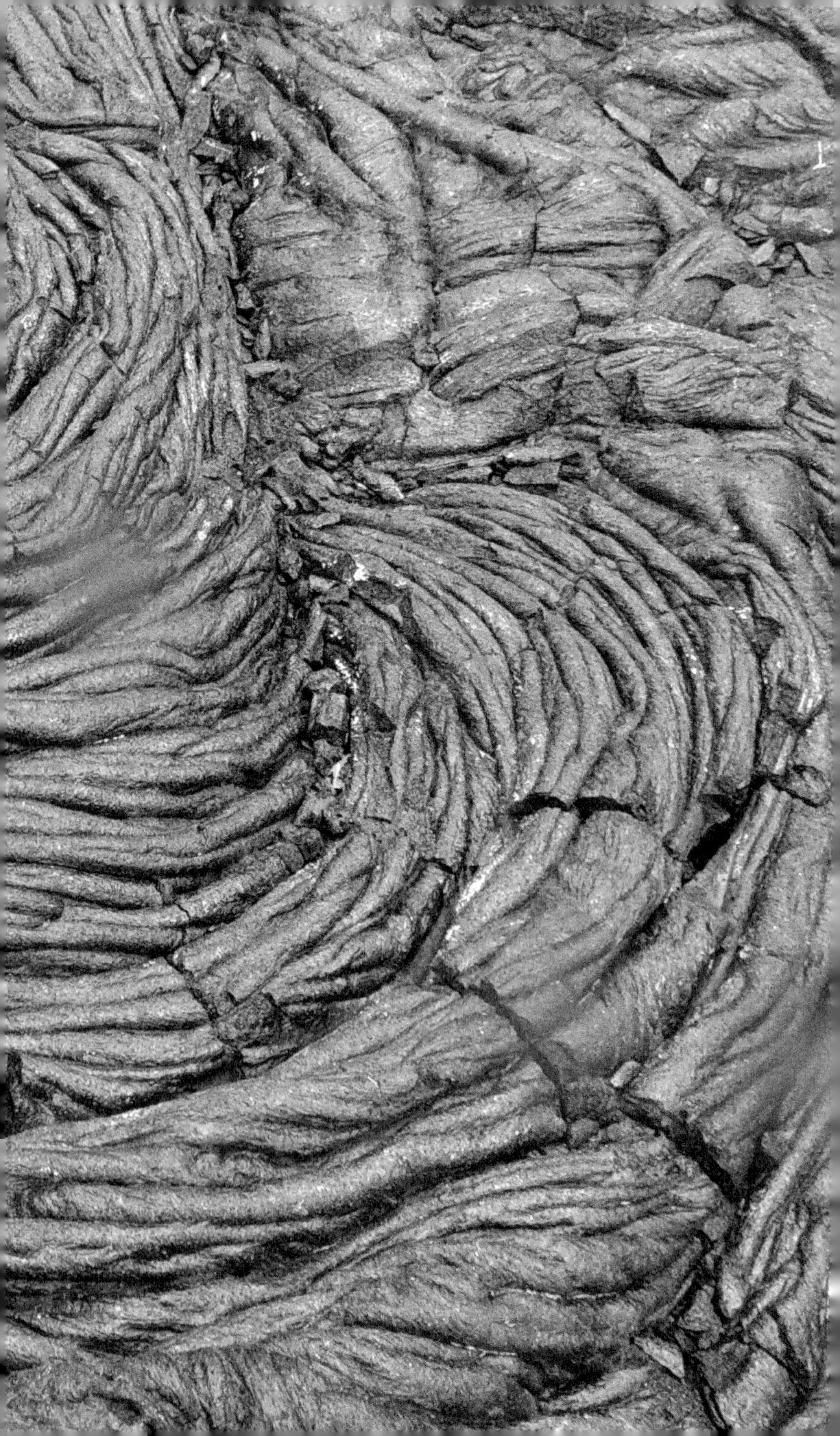

7. The most magnificent experiment of all times

Are you familiar with a man named Claus Jönsson? No? Well, in this case, we do have something in common because until recently, I did not know who he was, although I can still remember his experiment years after completing my studies of physics.

In 2002, "Physics World," the British Physics Alliance, conducted a survey among 200 physicists just to answer a single question: what is the most magnificent physics experiment of all times? An experiment that dated back to 1961 came in first and managed to beat even Galileo's and Newton's experiments. This experiment proves the correctness of quantum physics.

Which criteria would you use to assess the beauty of a physics experiment? According to the scientists who were actually interviewed, such an experiment has to be easy to visualize and verifiable. Moreover, it should also change the thinking and behavior patterns of mankind—so, quite a tall order.

While the survey participants were familiar with the experiment, most of them had no clue who the man behind the winning experiment was. It was quite a departure from the other top ranking experiments, such as Galileo's "Equations for a falling body," which is still frequently performed at modern-day schools. The outcome of the survey was surprising, because until then, Claus Jönsson, whose experiment had placed first was an unknown even to most of the experts who participated.

However, before we get to the actual experiment, I'd like to describe another experiment first. Why? Well—just be patient. You will uncover the reason soon enough.

An experiment with soccer balls

Now I want you to imagine a soccer field adjacent to a building that is sitting right next to the goal. Given that the balls being aimed at the goal frequently miss their target, the windows of the building obviously require some protection. Hence, the officials in charge at the soccer club have decided to erect a wooden picket fence right behind the goal to prevent the windowpanes from getting smashed in. I agree with what you're thinking right now: a chain-link fence would probably have been a better solution, but using wood panels makes it easier to explain our experiment. As a result of the frequent assaults the fence had to withstand from oncoming soccer balls, two of the panels had been broken out, which allowed the ball to pass through. The all-important question: Will the clubhouse's windowpane located right behind the picket fence still be protected?

From the bird's eye view, an inspection of the fence and the soccer field reveals the following situation:

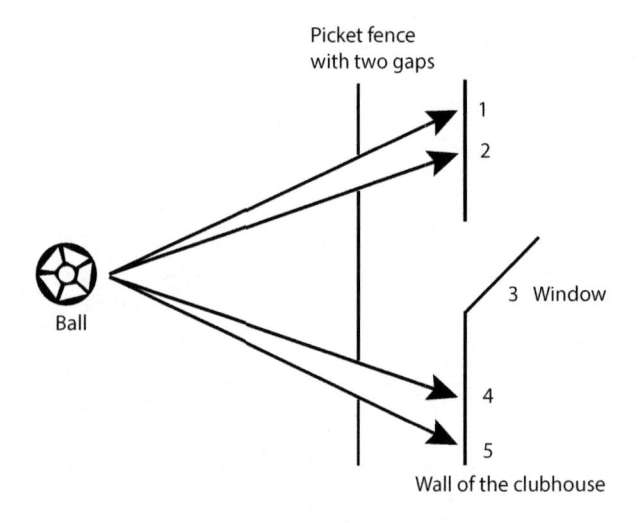

Figure 3: Double-slit experiment with soccer balls

If the soccer ball is sent flying through the left gap of the picket fence by a player from the eleven-meter-mark, the ball will hit the wall between positions 1 and 2. However, if the ball is catapulted through the right-hand gap, it can only hit the wall of the building behind it between positions 4 and 5. Hence, the window (position 3) cannot be broken by the shots aimed at the goal, given that the protective fence prevents a direct connection between the eleven-meter-mark and the window.

Now let's repeat the experiment with small particles. Instead of balls, we use electrons. Imagine the electrons to be tiny balls that cannot be divided into any smaller particles (elementary particles).

Jönsson's experiment

So we have now arrived at the point where we get to try the most magnificent experiment of all times, which, as previously mentioned, has been attributed to Claus Jönsson. It is called the double-slit experiment with electrons. The name is based on the number of open gaps (slits). This is actually the same experiment as the one performed above using the soccer balls, except that this one uses tiny particles. Instead of the ball, a source of electrons is used, which shoots out the electrons (a beam of many electrons). This process is the same as the one the soccer player performs when he directs the ball at the goal.

In this experiment, the wall of the club building is replaced by a screen, which is used to track and count the number of landing electrons. A grate is set up between the source of electrons and the screen, which has two openings in the form of narrow slits. Hence, the grate assumes the role of the picket fence with the two gaps. Do not be confused by the use of the term "grate". It's the official physics term, which is why I used it here.

In our case, you can picture the grate as a wall with two tiny openings in it.

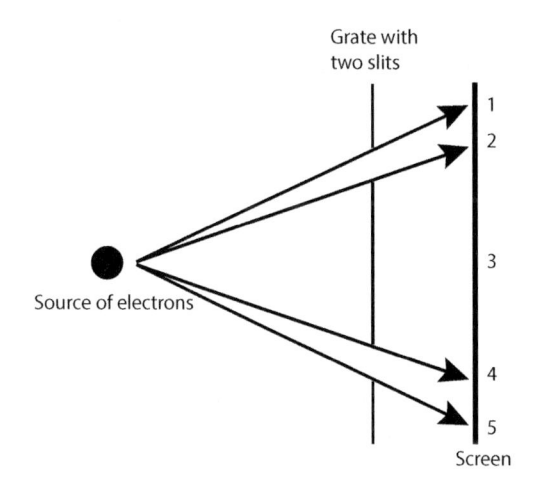

Figure 4: Double-slit experiment with electrons

So far, so good. At a first glance you will observe nothing spectacular. In fact, we should likely expect this experiment with the electrons to produce similar results to the one conducted with soccer balls. However, the experiment delivers a confusing result.

Most of the electrons hit the screen in position 3. This is the exact location where the window to be protected is located in our soccer ball example. So, in the electron experiment, no electrons at all should come into contact with the screen in this location, because a direct connection between the source of electrons and position 3 on the screen does not exist. Overall, what we get is a pattern of many bright and dark stripes akin to the patterns on zebra, whereby the main stripe, which is located on position 3, is the brightest one of all. Bright means lots of electrons; dark means no registered electrons. The further we move away from the middle (position 3), the fewer electrons hit the screen when compared to the main stripe.

Let's recap the situation: in the case of the soccer balls, there are only two areas of contact. In the electrons scenario, on the other hand, there are a lot of areas where the electrons can travel behind the two slits (gaps).

This result may surprise you. If so, you are in the same boat as the scientists who first conducted this experiment. While these researchers were very familiar with the stripe pattern, they knew it only in the context of overlapping waves—the ones we studied in our light experiment earlier in this book. However, in this case we are dealing exclusively with particles. How can this be?

It is possible to explain the result of this experiment if we presume that waves start in every slit. If two wave crests meet on the monitoring screen, they amplify and form the bright stripes. If, on the other hand, a wave crest and a wave trough come together, they nullify each other and form a dark stripe. That's exactly what we have learned from our light experiments.

Although only individual electrons, i.e. locally restricted small particles have been consistently measured on the monitoring screen, the sum total of all electrons acts like waves. However, when measuring on the monitoring screen, the individual particles are always located in just one specific position and never simultaneously in several locations. Waves, on the other hand, have a completely different character: they appear in several locations at the same time. Picture this: you're on the beach and the waves are moving in. They always come in across the entire length of the coastline, not just in the small area where you just happen to be sitting in a beach chair.

After the discovery of the electron's strange wave-particle behavior, physicists did try to find a reasonable explanation for this phenomenon. One of the ideas they came up with was that the crowding of all the electrons being directed at the grate created the waves. A good example for this effect: sound waves. They are generated by fluctuations in pressure, which cause more or less crowding among the air molecules. If the air molecules did not bang against each other and transmit sound waves as a result, it would not be possible to transmit noise and we would not be able to communicate with each other verbally.

Based on the above, it was presumed that the electron particles—just like the air particles—have an affect on each other when they crowd together in the slits during their flight and bang against each other. This could trigger a wave phenomenon. One thing that is important to remember is that these are waves that have been generated by particles consisting of matter. Such an explanation would still be congruent with traditional physics—the teachings we are familiar with from our everyday lives and which we have discussed in the first Chapter based on the pool billiards example.

To determine whether the wave effect is actually the result of crowding, scientists decided to conduct the double-slit experiment with single electrons. To do this, the particles were sent through the slit one by one to make sure they could no longer collide. First, one electron was sent on its journey. Before the next particle was allowed to take off, it had to wait until the first one had arrived on the monitoring screen. The positions of the individual electrons colliding with the screen were recorded and the experiment continued with several electrons over a period of time.

The all-important question is: does this experiment still produce the typical wave pattern of bright and dark stripes after an extended period of time? The answer: Yes! That's a huge surprise. Scientists repeated the experiment countless times and the result was always the same. Hence, there is complete consensus among physicists that the result is correct—no doubt about it.

This means that the behavior of electrons is just as paradox as the behavior of light. When they fly through two slits, they act just like waves and produce a striped pattern that is typical for waves on the monitoring screen. However, if measurements of them are taken on that very same monitoring screen, they can be registered as small particles. So what are they, really? Waves or particles? Or both? At the same time? These would be contradicting characteristics because a particle can always be found in one exact location and not simultaneously in multiple places. Waves, on the other hand, are expanded, penetrate through each other and can be found in several places simultaneously. They do not collide like particles do. The two ideas are the complete opposite of each other.

So let's dig a little deeper. Obviously, the electron is an individual particle at the beginning of the experiment. During flight, it converts into an expanded wave that passes through both slits at the same time. During this phase, the wave of the individual electron interacts with itself. At the end of the phase, the electron wave converts back into exactly one particle, which is measured precisely in one location on the monitoring screen.

You may wonder whether this explanation can even be taken seriously in conjunction with natural science. Well, the physicists thought so as well, which is why they placed a measuring device behind the two splits to verify through which slit the electron had passed. For the purpose of visualization, this was as if someone used some kind of flashlight to check which slit the respective electron slipped through.

The outcome was mind-boggling: the interference pattern with its many bright and dark stripes, which is so typical of waves, disappeared completely and was replaced by only two visible stripes that were equally bright. Hence, in the situation we observed, the electrons did not behave like waves any longer, but acted like particles. At this point, they were only registered in two areas—just like it had been the case in our soccer ball model. It appears as if the electrons knew that they were being observed.

Now let's get back to the original question: what actually is an electron? A particle or a wave? The answer: It depends on whether it is being observed or not. The electron acts like a particle as soon as one—for the purpose of visualization—checks which slit it has slipped through. If one does this, one can claim with absolute certainty that the electron passed through just one slit and not through both at the same time. If, on the other hand, one does not observe the electron, it behaves like a wave that has passed through both slits simultaneously. From a mathematical perspective the electron, prior to be being observed, exists in a state where all possibilities overlap. Hence, there is a possibly that it will travel through the left-hand slit; another option is that it passes through the right-hand slit and it may of course also pass through both slits or not travel through a slit at all. All of these options exist in what the experts call a superposition. The physicist defines this term to mean that all options for an overlapping state-like situation exist until the electron is ultimately observed. As soon as it is observed, the expanded wave that describes the many options mysteriously disappears and a particle manifests itself in exactly one position in the space.

So does this mean that the world actually only exists when we pay attention to it? Does the noise a tree makes when it falls in the forest only exist if someone is listening? Heisenberg took a clear stance in the subject matter: from his perspective it does not make any sense to make any statements about electrons or other objects as long as they are not being observed. Hence, one can only say that the electron started at the source of the electron and later arrived in a certain location on the monitoring screen. It is not possible to talk about the existence of an electron and its location during the interim states. This is somewhat reminiscent of the legend of the Loch Ness Monster, whose head and tail are visible, but not the middle part of its body. It is not possible to arrive at any conclusions about the body parts located between the two.

The primordial source of matter is intangible

Do you recall the "poem" about Schrödinger's wave and its meaning? Born had arrived at the conclusion that these waves were of the kind that describe probabilities. Accordingly, the overlapping waves contain information about probabilities that define where the individual electron can land on the monitoring screen. The important point to remember is that it is not possible to make any statements as to the concrete location of an individual particle. However, one can calculate the areas in which most of the electrons will land. These locations are in the exact same areas where the bright stripes are located. The waves merely describe probabilities—they neither transport mass nor energy. All the probabilities are numbers without dimensions and therefore intangible (immaterial)! From that we conclude that the primordial source of our material world is actually intangible. Henceforth, we will refer to these intangible (immaterial) waves as quantum waves.

At this point, hearing such a statement in the context of rational natural science you might be somewhat flabbergasted. What may sound like the words of a mystic has actually been concluded from an experiment that can be repeated at any time and is therefore verifiable. Theology considers God the primordial source of everything that exists. Does that mean that the quantum waves are somehow related to God? We will attempt to find an answer to this question in Chapter 8.

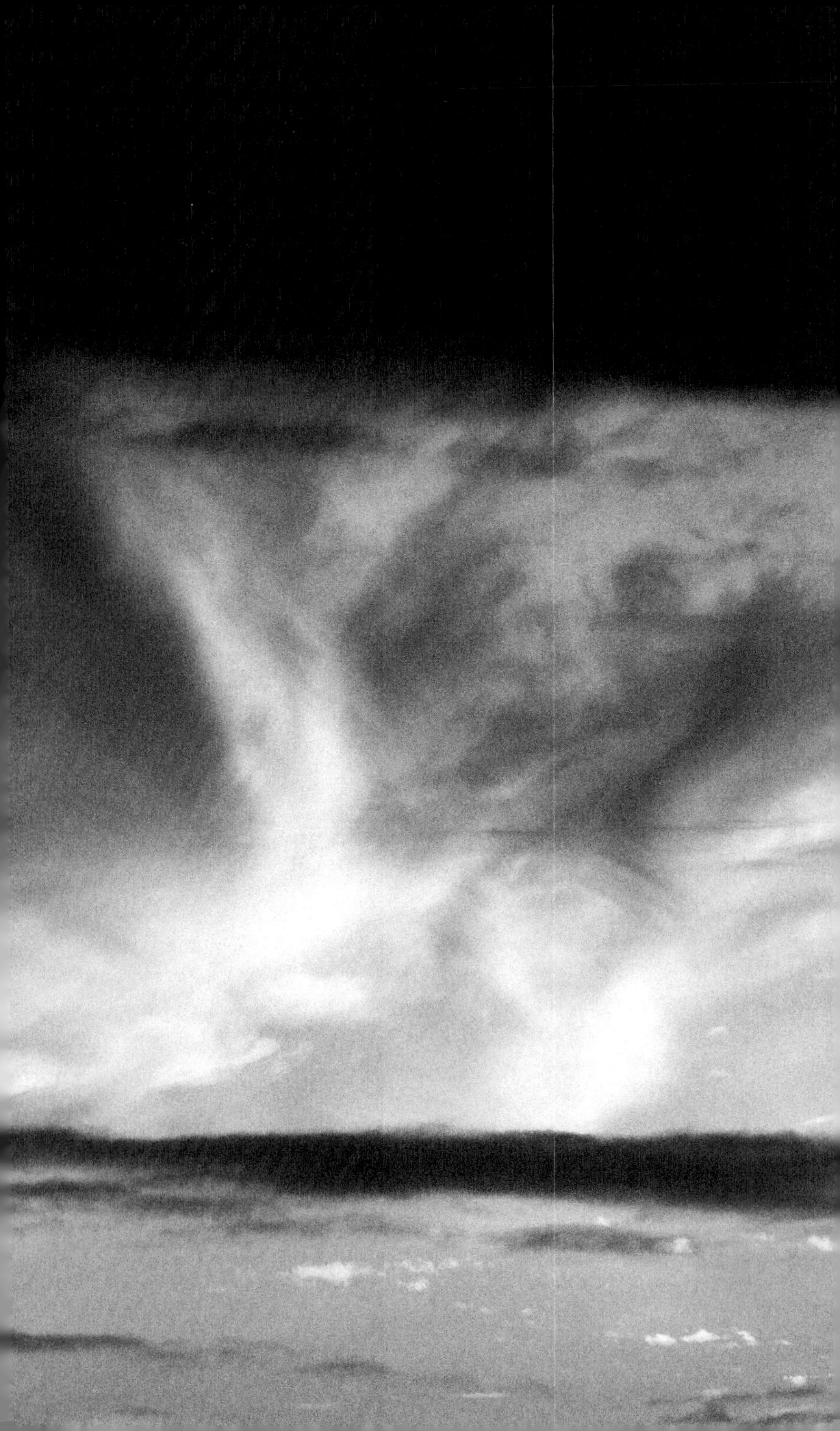

8. What do the terms "God" and "Heaven" mean?

We all get together for a Christmas celebration year after year. It's a wonderful tradition. We, in this case, means the staff and ex-employees of a large company who all worked in the same small branch in the past. After dinner, a former colleague and I began to talk about the book you are reading right now. He confided that he studies quantum physics during his time off and does so with great intensity. I was surprised since we had never even breached the subject before, although we'd worked in the same team for so many years and both shared a keen interest in the topic. We were just about to part ways when he quickly mentioned a book written by a theologian—a must read in his eyes. He urged me to get it. The title: *Einführung in das Christentum (Introduction to Christianity)*. It didn't sound particularly riveting to me. To be honest, I actually think the title is rather boring. Nevertheless, since I'd had quite a few "chance" encounters in the recent past that had given me new insights for my writing project, I decided to purchase the book all the same. And I certainly don't regret I did. I could hardly believe what I read in it with my own eyes:

"Erwin Schrödinger defined the structure of matter as wave packages . . .
However, the thought remains an enthralling parable . . . for the fact that
God, per se, is action and also for the fact that the densest existence—
God—exists in a majority of relationships, which are not substances but
nothing more than waves."

After I had read the quote a few times, I became conscious of the far-reaching consequences of this claim. After all, a highly renowned theologian is comparing God with the quantum waves as devised by Schrödinger. Moreover, this theologian considers these quantum waves a parable for God. Innumerable images of God do indeed exist, but it is certainly rather unconventional to compare Him with the quantum waves. You are probably familiar with this theologian's name—as he is—and I hope you're sitting down—none other than Joseph Ratzinger, the former Pope Benedict XVI. He wrote these thoughts down when he worked as a professor of theology at the University of Tübingen back in the 1960s.

Joseph Ratzinger's thoughts are definitely on par with what we have been able to devise from the results of the quantum physics experiments we have examined in this book. After all, as soon as the quantum world and its intangible waves become part of the equation, we find ourselves confronted with non-locality in space and time. These are the exact characteristics we can compare with the omnipresence and eternity of God. However, we will have to take into account that Joseph Ratzinger does not consider the quantum waves equal to God, but views them as a parable for God.

Which other impact might this parable have on our image of God? Well, the primordial source of all existence would be intangible because quantum waves cannot be explained on the basis of matter as evident from the results of the double slit experiment. They describe only those possibilities that allow tangible objects such as electrons to manifest during the taking of measurements or while being observed in our world. We will evaluate the difference between measuring and observing in the next Chapter. Either way, quantum waves are probability waves.

When we tried to identify the slit the individual electron slipped through, we destroyed the stripe pattern. Instead of many individual stripes, we only had two stripes left. The individual electron, while being observed, did not act like a wave any longer, but like a tangible particle. Obviously, it changed its behavior patterns as soon as we had information about its current location. In our normal everyday world, such behavior patterns would of course be absurd, since what we know or think about tangible objects does not influence them. What we do with them does. A cup sitting on the top of a table will not change its location because we know that it is full of coffee and we think its pretty. To get it to move, we have to lift it up or push it. However, things are different in quantum physics. As crazy as it may sound, the behavior of quantum systems is affected by what we know about them.

Yet it does not end there. Quantum objects behave as if they had minds. In his previously quoted book *Versteckte Wirklichkeit (Hidden Reality)*, physics professor Lothar Schäfer makes the following observations with regard to the quantums' strange behavior:

> "In normal reality, the ability to respond to information received is the
> privilege of the mind. Consequently, at the root of the material world,
> one discovers entities with mind-like characteristics and an intangible,
> non-energetic principle—information—as the effective cause of the effect."

Hence, the unobserved quantum waves, which describe all of the manifestation possibilities of elementary particles are mind-like as far as their characteristics are concerned. If we consider these exact quantum waves parables for God, God would be spirit by nature. The Bible corroborates this claim. The Book of John states:

"God is Spirit." (John 4.24)

Many other parts of the Bible refer to God's work as spiritual work. We will examine this aspect more thoroughly in Chapter 10.

From the physics perspective, we have devised that everything in this world has its roots in the quantum world, i.e. God. God is the origin of everything that is. While this would mean that everything is inherent in God, God would at the same time not be equivalent to the universe. On the one hand, only a part of the transcendent possibilities would be realized and on the other hand, we would never be able to observe the original form of the quantum waves. As soon as we attempt this, the waves convert themselves into actual tangible objects in our world. We cannot envision the likeness of God because He is transcendent and not of this material world.

John 18:36
Jesus said, "My kingdom is not of this world. . . . But now my kingdom is from another place."

So does the fact that God is transcendent mean that He is separate from our world? Before we address this question, I need to ask you to be patient a little longer since we do still need some very important information before we tackle this issue in greater detail.

The quantum waves dictate a structure that defines how something can manifest itself in our world in a tangible way. They describe the probability at which frequency certain incidents will occur. Nonetheless, they do not allow us to come to any conclusions about the individual events. Only the average result across numerous incidents can be projected in advance. Hence, the quantum waves are not just possibility waves, but also probability waves—just like we have seen in the coin tossing example. It is not possible to predict on which side the coin will land for just a single throw. However, it is possible to calculate that if coins are tossed many times, the coin will land on the coat of arms about half the time and on the number the other half of the time. This means that the individual case is subject to the freedom of randomness (2 Corinthians 3.17: *"Now the Lord is the Spirit, and where the Spirit of the Lord is, there is freedom."*);

however, the entirety of all incidents is subject to the rules of a mathematical-physical order. It ensures that our everyday lives—contrary to the quantum world—are ruled by deterministic natural laws on which we can accurately rely. However, the only reason this works is because we are dealing with a whole slew of quantum incidents that create the everyday world we can experience. For instance, it is thanks to these physical laws that we do not drop into the center of the earth.

We can consider the world of quantum waves with its probabilities and laws as God's order, which—at the same time - guarantees us freedom and dependability. How do we comprehend this Godly order? In the quantum physics interpretation, the foundation of matter is comprised of quantum waves that deliver the information about possible elementary particles. Hence, the primary element of our world is information, not matter.

In the first few lines of the Book of John, we find the following statement:
"In the beginning was the Word, and the Word was with God, and the Word was God. He was with God in the beginning. Through him all things were made; without him nothing was made that has been made."

What is the purpose of words? As a rule, they are used to communicate information. Regardless of whether this happens in a face-to-face conversation between two people or if it appears in newspapers, on the radio, on television, via text message, Facebook, blogs or Twitter—the primary purpose of communication is to pass on information. This makes me think that it is certainly proper to use the term "word" in a way comparable to the term "information."

As soon as we do just that, we can interpret the first sentences of the Gospel of John using these statements:
"In the beginning there was Information and Information was with God, and God was Information. Through it all things were made; without it nothing was made that has been made."

Incidentally, the meaning is already inherent in the word "information." "In-formation" means to "bring something into a form." Everything that exists in our world has been previously created as potential in a transcendent, godly area beyond our world as information and is tangibly molded "into form."

How do the carbon atoms of a flower know where they have to position themselves to form the entire flower? The knowledge can only come from the quantum waves, which deliver this information. If you were to exchange your carbon atoms with those of a flower, you would still be the same person and the flower would remain the same flower. Hence, what counts is the information and not the matter. Information is more fundamental than matter.

So are these waves of information static and immobile? Do they retain the same form for all times and do they always describe the same possibilities? Or do they change all the time? The use of Schrödinger's Equation as a helpful tool reveals that the waves do in fact change all the time and that they are alive. Consequently—if we consider the waves parables for God—the God we are talking about is alive and not an immovable mover (Aristotle).

The letters we find in the Gospel of Paul, which describes God as the "living God", also corroborates our claim, which was devised from quantum physics. For instance in 2 Corinthians, 3.3:

"You are a letter of Christ written not with ink but with the Spirit of the living God, not on tablets of stone but on tablets of human hearts."

However, Jeremiah 10.10 also makes this reference to God:
"But the LORD is the true God; he is the living God and the everlasting King."

Perhaps you might be at a loss of what to do with the image of a living God. Here on earth being alive means that we breathe, eat, walk around and talk to other humans. So what does the expression "living God" really mean? Well, we could work around this and apply the term "living" to Jesus, who is considered the Son of God. However, this is not what the term refers to in our case. The quantum waves are transcendent and cannot be compared to tangible objects in our world.

Nonetheless we can envision a living God. After all, He responds to our observations of the world. Let's recap: When we determine the slit the electron has passed through in the double slit-experiment, the generated stripe pattern changes. God responds to our observation by converting the transcendent quantum wave into something tangible—an electron—at the moment we begin to observe. This reaction to an action is definitely one of the characteristics of being alive. Sentient beings encounter each other and exhibit certain behaviors that are usually affected by the actions of the other sentient being. Objects such as tables, chairs, cups and cabinets do not do this. If you talk to a table it will not act any differently; in fact, it will always stay where it is. Hence, we are automatically in constant communication with God although we are perhaps not even aware of it. Without this connection our world would cease to exist.

Now let's briefly recap what we have so far devised from a natural science perspective from the quantum waves, which are considered parables for God.

God . . .
Is non-local from the time perspective (non-local in time), i.e. eternal
Is geographically non-local (non-local in space), i.e. omnipresent
Is transcendent, i.e. not of this world
Is the primordial source for all there is
Is spirit
Means freedom
Means that our world is governed by a Godly order
Is information
Is alive
Is constantly communicating with us

What is Heaven?

"In the beginning God created the heavens and the earth" says Genesis 1.1. All kinds of visions come to mind when we try to interpret the term "Heaven." Either way, it plays a central and prominent role in the faith of many people.

God is the one who resides in Heaven. It is not accessible and identifiable for us. Earth, on the other hand, is our familiar habitat; the one we have been entrusted with and live in. Hence, we have to make a clear distinction between these two zones.

Is it possible to use quantum physics as a basis for something we could use to define Heaven and earth? If we once again presume that the quantum waves are the terrain of God, they are transcendent and therefore inaccessible and not measureable. Our stance is congruent with the statements in the Bible as far as this is concerned. However, from the perspective of natural science, we can say something more about Heaven. Heaven comprises all of the possibilities of what can materialize here on earth. At a first glance this may appear to be a somewhat unconventional and extraordinary approach. However, if one does some research, one will eventually find theologians who share this understanding. One of today's most renowned theologians is Prof. Dr. Jürgen Moltmann. In his book *Gott in der Schöpfung (God in Creation)*, he corroborates this concept, although he does not link it to quantum physics. Prof. Dr. Jürgen Moltmann is considered one of the world's most acclaimed theologians, who has been awarded numerous honorary doctorates and awards. Among his achievements are numerous awards from universities in the United States, England, Scotland, Holland and Romania. Among others, he received the Grawemeyer Award in Religion from the University of Louisville, Kentucky, USA in 2000, which included $200,000 in prize money.

In his book *Gott in der Schöpfung (God in Creation)*, Jürgen Moltmann writes:
"The term 'Heaven' refers to the sphere of God's creative abilities and powers.... The term "earth" designates the place of created reality.... All recognizable processes indicate that there are interrelations between reality and possibility. Potential realities eventually turn into possibilities that have materialized."

This is exactly what we found out in our investigation of quantum theory. The possibilities described by the quantum waves (possible realities) evolve into actual tangible objects (created reality). This describes the process of creation from the perspective of quantum physics. To use the language of the Bible, the conversion of possibilities into matter represents the Word of God in the flesh. It is the likeness of the invisible God. The invisible (possibility waves) is the pattern for the visible.

The pattern itself is intangible. This is hard to imagine since we are used to always linking a pattern to something tangible. It might be helpful to use an example, Heisenberg's protégé and Alternative Nobel Prize winner Hans-Peter Dürr brought up in one of his presentations. Did you ever wonder how it is even possible for you to talk to a far away friend over your cell phone? The answer: this is possible because patterns are being transmitted. As soon as you begin to talk into your cell phone, your words are converted into patterns and transmitted to your friend's cell phone. The information transmitted in the form of patterns is converted back into words once his device receives it.

Yes, it is mind-boggling indeed. Although we approached the subject matter from two different angles—the theological end and from the perspective of natural science, we have arrived at the same conclusion as to how the world was and is still being created: through the conversion of transcendent possibilities into matter.

So who or what chooses the actual event from all of these possibilities? Do we? Is it God? Or does God make the selection along with us? The next few Chapters will thoroughly investigate this enthralling topic.

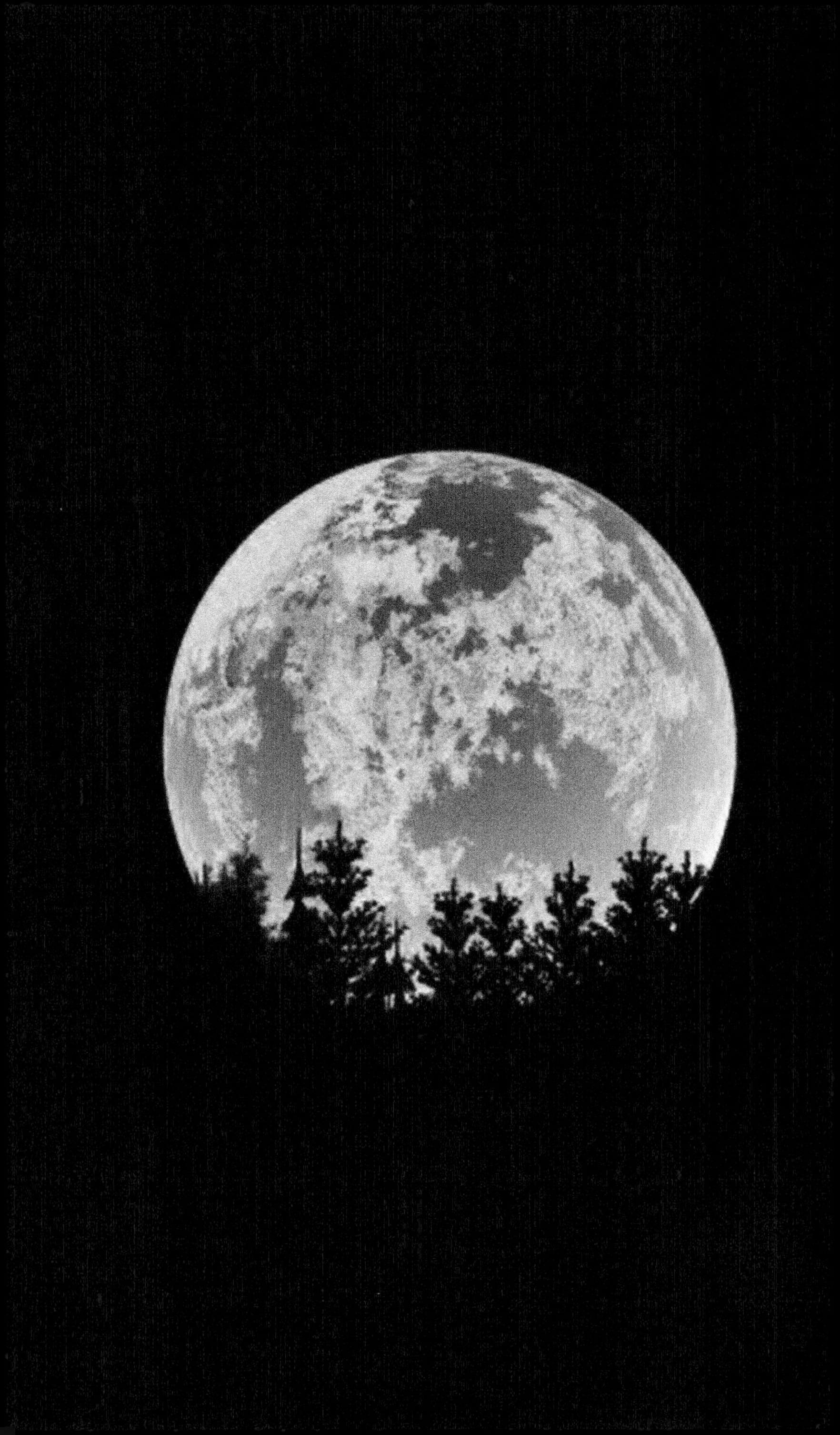

9. Does the moon exist even if no one is looking?

"Then my turn came, fourth to be sent from the room so that Lothar Nordheim's other fifteen after-dinner guests could consult in secret and agree on a difficult word. I was locked out unbelievably long. On finally being readmitted, I found a smile on everyone's face; a sign of a joke or a plot. I nevertheless started my attempt to find the word. "Is it animal?" "No." "Is it mineral?" "Yes." "Is it green?" "No." "Is it white?" "Yes." These answers came quickly. Then the questions began to take longer in the answering. It was strange. All I wanted from my friends was a simple yes or no. Yet the one queried would think and think, yes or no, no or yes, before responding. Finally I felt I was getting hot on the trail; that the word might be "cloud." I knew I was allowed only one chance at the final word. I ventured it: "Is it cloud?" "Yes," came the reply and everyone burst out laughing. They explained to me there had been no word in the room. They had agreed not to agree on a word. Each one questioned could answer as he pleased—with the one requirement that he should have a word in mind compatible with his own response and all that had gone before. Otherwise, if I challenged, he lost. The surprise version of the game of twenty questions was therefore as difficult for my colleagues as it was for me."

This story is a parable renowned physicist John Wheeler, who came up with the Delayed Choice Experiment, told his audience when he tried to explain the crazy conclusions of quantum physics in a way people could understand. The Story has been recited from the book *The Ghost in the Atom* by authors Davies and Brown. So how is any of that related to quantum physics? To find the answer to this question—and I must apologize for reverting back to this experiment so frequently—we once again will consult the double-slit experiment. We have aimed electrons at two narrow slits and have received a pattern of bright and dark stripes on the other end. We explained that this happened due to overlapping quantum waves. Curiously, the electrons we fired off, began their journey as particles and turned into quantum waves in-flight once they had taken off, only to convert themselves back into particles in the end after landing on the monitoring screen. A crazy story. Strangely enough, the individual electron travels simultaneously through both slits as a quantum wave and impacts itself. We have shown this by sending off individual electrons one by one so that they could not affect each other by way of collision.

Nevertheless, after some time, the pattern typical for waves appeared on the monitoring screen as a result of the individual particles landing on it. The individual electron always appears on the screen as a spot in a certain location. It cannot be predicted where the individual particle will land. Nonetheless, it is possible to compute the entire stripe pattern with the assistance of quantum mechanics. Wherever bright stripes appear, it is highly likely that we will register an electron.

In traditional physics, one general rule is that we can project the flight paths of objects with perfect precision. When we shoot a pistol and aim the bullet at the target, we can predict precisely where the bullet will hit. To do this, all we need to know are the starting parameters, such as the speed, firing angle and the ambient conditions. However, when we perform the double-slit experiment with electrons we can only calculate probabilities and cannot make predictions for the individual electron—not even if we know exactly what the starting parameters are.

The coin toss situation is a similar scenario. While we cannot predict on which side the coin will land, we do know that if many tosses take place, half of them will land on the number and the other half on the coat of arms. Hence the odds of getting the number or the coat of arms are 50:50.

Nonetheless, the comparison with the coin toss is problematic as far as one aspect is concerned because we could theoretically project precisely on which side the coin will land as long as we know the exact initial conditions. The problem with computing the result is this: if these initial conditions change only slightly, we might get a completely different result.

How a butterfly can trigger a hurricane

You may have heard someone make the claim that a butterfly batting its wings in the Amazon region can trigger a hurricane in the United States some time later. This story can be attributed to the so-called chaos theory, which asserts that even small changes in the initial conditions can lead to major changes of events.

This is one example that corroborates the fact that we are not in a position to concisely project the behavior of chaotic systems. However, let's presume just once that we do have the capacity to precisely know every butterfly's movements and the other influences of the world and that we can take them into account in our computations. This would enable us to forecast the weather with absolute certainty. This, however, is not possible in quantum physics. The reason: Werner Heisenberg's Uncertainty Principle, which—you guessed it—we have already discussed in Chapter 2 in conjunction with some of the Coen Brothers' movies. Amit Goswami, a physicist with an East Indian-American background, who taught as a professor at the University of Oregon, commented on this in his book *The Self-Aware Universe*:

"According to the Uncertainty Principle, we cannot simultaneously determine with certainty both the position and the velocity (or momentum) of an electron; any effort to measure one accurately blurs our knowledge of the other. Thus the initial conditions for the calculation of a particle's trajectory can never be determined with accuracy, and the concept of a sharply defined trajectory of a particle is untenable."

Therefore, the big difference between a classic theory such as chaos theory and the quantum theory is as follows: In conventional physics teachings, such as chaos theory, our uncertainties about the movements of an object stem merely from the fact that we do not know the exact initial conditions, while they are fundamental in nature in quantum physics given that the initial conditions cannot even be precisely defined because of the Uncertainty Principle.

Quantum physics comprises four key fundamental principles:

1. *Wave function (quantum wave)*: Every quantum object is mathematically described by a wave function. It is intangible. It exists neither in space nor time, nor does it consist of matter or energy. Thus, it is a kind of spiritual information wave. This wave function also describes the movement of objects.

2. *Possibilities:* Each quantum object that is described by the wave function has the capability to only manifest itself in one specific location in the everyday world we are familiar with. Prior to being measured/observed, the quantum object has many positioning options. Ultimately, because of the measurement/observing activity, only one of these many possibilities comes to fruition, so that the particle ends up in just one exact location in the room/space in our actual world.

3. *Measurement/Observation (we will evaluate what the difference is in more detail later in this book)*: The measuring/observation action makes

one concise choice from the possibilities set forth in Section 2 and converts this exact choice into a tangible object that can be found in our world.

4. *Probability*: Probability is the term used to describe the frequency with which a certain possibility manifests itself as a result of the measurement/observing action. It is calculated with the assistance of the wave function (Section 1).

Reverting back to our coin toss example, the possibilities are the coat of arms or the number (Section 2). The probability of one of the two options to manifest itself is 50:50 (Section 4). The tossing of the coin (Section 3) is equivalent to the measuring/observing action in this case. Unfortunately, the wave function cannot be compared to this model at all. This is where we reach the limitations of the parable. Given that the wave function is extremely unique, we will cover it in detail below.

So let's look at the example of a crate into which someone has placed a marble. We have not observed this process. Now we insert separating walls into the center of the crate to divide it into two halves. It's basically the same thing that happens in the famous magic trick where the assistant is locked into a crate, which is subsequently cut in two pieces.

We bring one half of the crate to New York, while the other half is transported to San Francisco. Where is the glass marble at this point? We cannot predict the outcome with certainty since we did not see where in the crate the marble was initially placed. However, what we can claim with certainty is that it definitely was in one of the two halves the entire time while traveling to San Francisco or New York. We can determine the location of the glass marble by simply opening one of the two halves. The probability that it is in one of the two cities is 50:50.

Now let's repeat this same experiment using a quantum object (e.g. an electron), which we will lock up in a container with impenetrable walls. Just like with the glass marble, we will split it into two halves. Once again, we'll transport one half to New York and the other to San Francisco. Following the definition in traditional physics there is no difference between this experiment and the one with the glass marble.

However, in quantum physics, the experiment presents itself in a completely different light than in traditional physics. So, what does happen if we divide the container and send one half to San Francisco and the other to New York? Wave function mathematics dictates that the electron is simultaneously in both container halves, i.e. in New York and San Francisco at the same time. However, as we dig deeper, the whole story becomes even harder to believe. The wave function also says that the electron is in neither one of the two container halves and may also just be in one of them. All of these different options exist simultaneously as what scientists call a superposition (overlapping situation). This remains true until a measurement is taken and the electron "decides" on one half and actually materializes in it. The proper way to describe this is that the electron, pre-measurement, is in a situation in which it does not make sense to query where it is located. In other words, asking this question would be akin to asking a cheese sandwich for its political affiliation. One could certainly ask the question, but it wouldn't make any sense to do so.

Prior to the performance of a measurement, electrons do not exist—neither in space nor in time. Hence, one can say that elementary particles, such as the electrons are not actually real while they are not being observed and that their actual existence is the result of our observation. Werner Heisenberg had the following to say about this in his book *Physik und Philosophie (Physics and Philosophy; 1958)*:

"In atomic operation experiments we are dealing with objects and facts, with occurrences that are just as real as they are in everyday life. However, the atoms or elementary particles are not real in the same way. They are more likely to form a world of tendencies or possibilities than one consisting of objects and facts."

Let's revert back to the story at the beginning of this Chapter: what does it want to tell us? A world that hinges on observation does not exist out there; in fact, reality does not manifest itself until we ask our questions, make our observations and take our measurements. In the story, the one posing the questions presumed that the other party guests had agreed upon a term in advance. This, however, was not the case, as the word did not evolve until he began to pose questions. If he had asked different questions, it is likely that a different word would have emerged. In other words, an objective reality that exists out there and is not contingent upon our observations does not exist.

In this context, Einstein provokingly asked: "Does the moon even exist if no one is looking?" From the perspective of quantum physics

Heisenberg represents, the logical response would be "No." The reason: the moon itself is composed of quantum objects that are not real prior to being observed. Hence, the moon does not exist in the absence of observation. This is difficult for us and also many physicists to wrap our heads around. This is why scientists still have not come to an agreement on the matter even as we speak.

You may now have arrived at the conclusion that the whole thing doesn't have anything to do with natural science at this point. If you feel that way, Niels Bohr, one of the era's leading quantum physicists, would agree with you. He, Heisenberg, Pauli, Schrödinger and other developed and interpreted the discipline of quantum physics. Niels Bohr summed it up in this statement:

Anyone who is not shocked by quantum theory has not understood it.

In the 1920s, Bohr had established and developed an institute in Copenhagen, where the entire world's leading quantum physicists convened. It was the venue where the Copenhagen Interpretation of Quantum Physics was developed, which attempts to explain the collapse of the wave function—i.e. the conversion of possibilities into facts.

Perhaps you are now wondering what or who it is that makes the wave function collapse. Or, to put it in a different context: who or what converts the possibilities into actual objects in our material world? Unfortunately, very few physicists actually research this very critical quantum physics problem.

Why is the number of natural scientists who actually take an interest in this very elementary question of the structure and evolution of matter so small? Well, for most of them, the interpretation of quantum physics is irrelevant for their daily work. It is in fact possible to use the Schrödinger Equation to develop high tech devices such as magnetic resonance tomography without even giving the collapse of the wave function a second thought. Even physics study courses usually allocate very little time to the interpretation of quantum physics. As long as quantum mechanics (the mathematical term used to describe quantum physics) provide us with a highly dependable tool that allows us to project the results of experiments, this is apparently not necessary. What counts is that new technical applications are developed for corporations that help them boost their revenues and profits. The actual acquisition of new insights somehow seems to be dispensable. This is an attitude that has become typical for our day and age. Yet you and I will not be sidetracked and will focus in detail on the all important quantum physics question: Who or what causes the wave function to collapse?

The collapse of the wave function cannot be explained on the basis of either the mathematical description of quantum physics or of any experiments. Various theories aiming to resolve the problem have been developed. However, in my opinion an interpretation that would explain the measurement problem—i.e. the conversion of intangible possibilities into actual tangible objects completely free of paradoxes has not been provided to date—with one exception. We will now take a close look at this solution.

Even though innumerable different interpretations of quantum physics exist today, the Copenhagen Interpretation developed by Heisenberg and Bohr remains the official interpretation, which appears most frequently in textbooks. Based on the Copenhagen Interpretation, three fundamental answers to the question who or what causes the wave function to collapse are currently available.

The measuring device

The original version of the Copenhagen Interpretation presumes that a measurement causes the wave function (the mathematical description of the quantum wave) to collapse. This begs the question: What is a measurement? To perform one, we first and foremost need a measuring device, for instance a detector like the one we used in the earlier described experiments. This device performs the measurement on the quantum system. For example, it registers where the electron manifests itself materially.

Contrary to the tiny objects—electrons, other elementary particles and atoms—there are also larger objects we encounter in our everyday lives. Tables, chairs, bottles, balls, cups, computers and measuring devices all belong in this category. We call this sphere the macrocosm. Unlike the microscopic objects that do not occupy a firmly defined position in the room/space, macroscopic objects are always located in a specific position in the room. For instance, the vase holding roses will usually sit on the center of the table and not in several other places at the same time. Quantum objects, on the other hand, are distributed across the entire room, space and the entire universe—in the form of wave functions.

The Copenhagen Interpretation approaches the issue by strictly separating the macroscopic and the microscopic world. Hence, it positions the macroscopic measuring device outside of the sphere of microscopic quantum physics. This, however, is a huge problem for us. After all, the measuring device itself is a system composed of quantum objects such as atoms and electrons—i.e. intangible quantum worlds. If one couples such a measuring device with the quantum objects to be measured, this only enlarges the structure of possibilities described by the quantum waves and does not convert them into tangible objects. Possibility interlinked with possibility only creates even more possibilities and never an actual tangible object.

Another idea one might devise at this point is to monitor the measuring device and the quantum object to be measured through a second measuring device. Would this resolve our problem? No, it would not because it would only further expand the entire quantum system of possibilities. Even an endless chain of measuring devices would not be able to cause the collapse of the wave function. In physics, one refers to this concept as the "von Neumann Chain", a system named for mathematician von Neumann. No matter how hard we try—possibility coupled with possibility will always only deliver more possibilities, never actuality. So the problem remains.

The consciousness of the observer

Von Neumann came up with the idea that a conscious observer—for instance a human being—could make the wave function collapse and therefore also stop the chain named for him. There are logical justifications that corroborate von Neumann's proposal. After all, every time we observe the electron, we see it as an actual tangible particle in a location and never in a scenario of multiple overlapped states (i.e. in the previously mentioned superposition) in several locations at the same time. Hence, it is von Neumann's claim that the wave function collapses and the superposition disappears as a result as soon as a conscious observer looks at the scenario.

So let's find out what consciousness (awareness) actually is and how it develops. Most brain researchers are of the opinion that the human brain generates consciousness in individuals. The brain is there first; the consciousness follows. What is the human brain comprised of? Protons, neutrons and electrons form atoms, which in turn produce molecules. The molecules form neurons, which provide the brain's structure and the brain generates consciousness. Well, that's quite a long chain. In other words, the primordial foundation of the world would be tangible and consists of elementary, tiny particles that cannot be divided any further and which form complicated entities until they ultimately generate the brain and hence, consciousness. This is how the world is perceived by materialism.

And what is quantum physics' stance as far as this logic is concerned? To that end, we will follow the arguments raised by quantum physicist Amit Goswami, as presented in his book *The Physicists' View of Nature*. Electrons, protons and neutrons consist of possibilities. Thus, possible electrons, protons and neutrons form possible atoms, which produce possible molecules, which in turn build possible neurons, which create a possible brain, which generates possible consciousness.

So is it possible for possible consciousness to convert a possible particle into an actual, tangible particle by causing the wave function to collapse? Is it possible that a coupling of possibility with possibility generates something real, i.e. something tangible? Well, let's examine this example a little more thoroughly in everyday life. Think about your next vacation trip. You want to pay for it. Let's presume you possibly have money in your account. Can you pay for your vacation with money you might possibly have? Unfortunately not. You can only use actual cash to pay for your vacation. Well, the other option would have been too good to be true.

Thus, if you combine possibility with possibility all you get is possibility and never something real. This means that the theory of the observer's consciousness causing the wave function to collapse simply does not work. In any event, this will not work if one considers consciousness as something that is generated by the brain as defined in materialism and which consists of tangible elementary particles.

So what about intangible consciousness? Right away, we run into yet another problem. This one's called dualism. Descartes introduced a distinction between mind and matter (spiritual and material substances) that are not related at all and that do not interact with each other. So how could intangible consciousness cause the wave function of a tangible object to collapse if the two are not affiliated with each other? In fact, from the physics perspective, this would be contingent upon an exchange of energy between the material and the spiritual world. However, all of the energy from the material world remains consistent and does not change. If an actual exchange in the form of energy with the intangible world were to happen, the physicists would long have discovered this in their experiments. However, this is not the case.

If this were not enough, there is yet another problem. What happens, if there are two observers who both simultaneously make the wave function collapse with the power of their minds and consciousness? U.S.-based Nobel Prize winner Eugene Wigner drew our attention to this problem. The observation was named "Wigner's Friend" in his honor.

Amit Goswami once again came up with an illustrative everyday example for the "Wigner's Friend" paradox: Two individuals—you and a good friend—simultaneously reach a multi-directional traffic intersection. A traffic light controls the movement of traffic at this crossroads. Given that you and your friend are both in a hurry and want to make sure you arrive at work punctually, each one of you wants to take advantage of the traffic light's green phase. So who'll get the green light? Who'll make the decision? Can you identify the upcoming paradoxes? Your individual states of consciousness—let's call them ego consciousness—want to cause the wave function to collapse to make sure that one of you gets the green light. However, the two options are in conflict with each other. So who chooses? The question remains unresolved.

Nonetheless, a solution for this problem does exist. The idea is that only your consciousness is real and creates everything that surrounds you. Only you are real. All objects and even all other people are being created exclusively by you. The movie *The 13th Floor*, which was shown in theaters in the late 1990s, explores this exact subject matter. The hero is a programmer who has created a virtual reality he can click into and out of as he chooses. It appears as if all of the other people who appear in it think and act as individuals and have no idea that they are only simulated characters. The story takes a surprising turn because the developer eventually discovers that he himself is a component of superior programming. Living in such a world would likely be a very depressing perspective.

The one omnipresent consciousness

Apparently, we get caught between a rock and a hard place whenever we try to explain the arising of reality based on natural science. Nonetheless, there is a surprising and logical answer that provides a solution for the measurement problem: we have to unfetter ourselves from our system of material reality and assume a consciousness that affects the former from the outside—one single consciousness This is the only solution that will ultimately allow us to resolve the measurement problem. This consciousness makes a selection from the numerous possibilities that the intangible quantum waves describe. It ensures that you and your friend will receive the same amount of green phases from the traffic light on average. This one consciousness can also ensure that you receive more green phases if the situation demands it. For instance, when an injured person has to be transported to the hospital as quickly as possible.

It causes the wave function to collapse and converts exactly one of the many possibilities into one real, tangible incident. How can it achieve this without sending signals through our universe attached with the known limitations of space and time and without exchanging energy? An exchange of energy between our material world and the world of transcendent quantum waves is redundant given that both spheres are components of the one consciousness. This consciousness makes its choice from its own possibilities, whereby it communicates without sending signals through space and time. This conclusion is essential in order to be able to explain the non-locality in space and time, which cannot be explained on the basis of the theory of relativity.

Consequently, on a primordial level, beneath the awareness of the individual, there is the one, non-local, omnipresent and universal consciousness that connects everything else, as we have been able to observe during our experiments with the entangled particles. Henceforth, we will refer to this one consciousness as quantum consciousness. As far as I know, Amit Goswami first introduced this term.

"Wait a minute," you might exclaim right now. After all, if this consciousness does in fact encompass all possibilities of the material world, why aren't all intangible possibilities converted into actual tangible objects? A justified question indeed. Given its non-locality, this one consciousness would be watching all possibilities at all times. Everywhere and constantly. The measurement problem of quantum physics can therefore not be resolved on the basis of the quantum waves and a sole and omnipresent conscience alone. It also takes an individual, tangible mind, like the one our brain creates. We call this individual mindfulness the ego mindfulness or the brain-mind. It is your own individual awareness that allows you to be aware of yourself and to experience your own individuality separately from all the other people and the entire world.

Let's recap: the collapse of the wave function, which consists of intangible quantum waves is caused by the one, non-local consciousness (quantum consciousness) with the support of a brain-mind. This concept was first devised by the previously introduced physicist Amit Goswami and resolves the measurement problem of quantum physics covered by this Chapter, which is still a controversial subject to this day, without any contradictions. Our next step in this process will be, to take this idea to the next level. After all, it is a striking fact that this triple-layer structure of intangible quantum waves, a non-local consciousness and a tangible brain-mind is reminiscent of a similar structure we are familiar with from the Bible—the Trinity of Father, Son and Holy Spirit. Is this happenstance or is it the gateway to a lot more? And most importantly: Will we find concrete parallels between the statements found in the Bible and those of quantum physics? We will examine these exciting questions more thoroughly from this point forward until the end of the book.

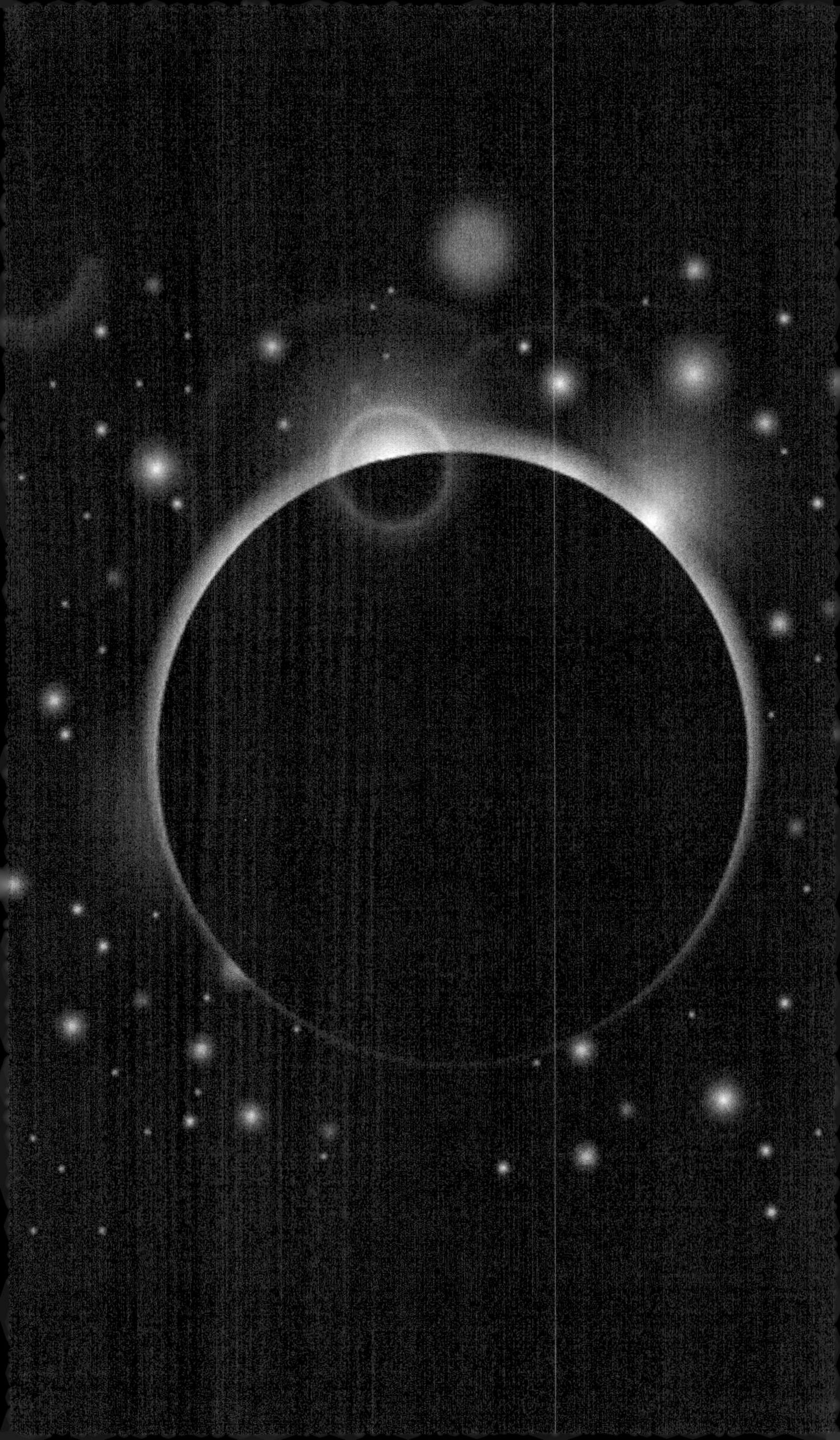

10. The secret of the Holy Spirit

In the previous Chapter, we devised the most important finding in this book so far—the one that describes the evolution of the reality in our world: the fact that the one, non-local consciousness (quantum consciousness) working in synchronicity with a brain-mind causes the collapse of the intangible wave function through conscious observation.

Based on this insight and a striking similarity with the Trinity, we are now formulating the following thesis, which we will investigate in more detail later in the book:

Quantum waves = Father
Quantum consciousness = Holy Spirit
Material brain-mind = Son

After all, Joseph Ratzinger already identified quantum waves as parables for God. Now we are also making the Holy Spirit and the Son part of the equation. We use the "equals" symbol like a parable—just like the former Pope did it. Our language, which is certainly quite colloquial—the language of apple pickers as the previously cited Heisenberg protégé Hans-Peter Dürr once referred to it in a presentation—is not the best when it comes to discussing our topic, because in our daily lives, we interact with objects we can literally grasp with our own hands. In other words, with material things. However, when we look beyond the boundaries of our material world, our colloquial language fails us, because it lacks the proper terms. We can only work with parables and imagery—just like Jesus did.

Based on the Bible, we will henceforth refer to this triple structure comprising quantum waves, quantum consciousness and the individual brain-mind, which we have devised from quantum theory, as the trinity of quantum physics.

So let's recap what we have learned so far. The material world we are familiar with can only be scientifically explained in a manner that is devoid of contradictions and paradoxes if we presume that there is a secret primordial source for the creation of all material and spiritual things, which we have referred to as the quantum waves. Although this source is intangible and transcendent, everything emerges from it—from the tiniest elementary particle to atoms, human beings, the stars and even the vastest of galaxies. Even if this subject has not come up until now, it is important to know that our thoughts and therefore all spiritual objects evolve from this primordial source of the quantum waves. One example of a spiritual object would be the action of thinking of a ball. The ball as such is of course a material object.

It is not possible for any sentient being to observe the primordial source in its original form. The reason is that whenever we watch the quantum waves, they become actual objects of our world. While it is possible to mathematically describe the quantum worlds with a tool called the Schrödinger Equation (= godly order, see Chapter 8); they will always remain hidden from us.

The primordial source, which remains completely concealed from us due to the strange characteristics of quantum theory, will, however, not suffice to explain the generation of our material world. It takes a single, non-local (eternal and omnipresent) quantum consciousness whose help is required to choose the actual material manifestations for our world from the quantum world. Ultimately, this one consciousness will result in the realization of just one of the possibilities among many options. In an interview conducted by Swiss Television, Hans-Peter Dürr once called this selection process "as mass murder of possibilities." This may sound bellicose, but the shoe fits. This one consciousness always gets help from a tangible (immanent) brain-mind when it chooses the possibility. To that end, it is critical that the wave function will collapse only if an individual brain-mind participates along with the quantum consciousness. If only the one consciousness were present and watches all possibilities all the time and everywhere, all options would come to fruition simultaneously. This, however, is not the case. Only one of the innumerable possibilities manifests itself each and every time.

At this point you may wonder why you are not aware of your connection with the quantum consciousness in your random everyday life. Why do we experience ourselves as individual "I-entities?" The reason: we are conditioned. We are impacted by our experiences and our past behaviors. This is also why we have limited leeway when it comes to making choices, since we do respond similarly to certain triggers all the time. Although we would actually have quite a few more choices, an ego consciousness limits our alternatives. If we were living quantum consciousness, we would have the freedom to randomly choose from a variety of options the quantum waves offer us.

The actual choices made from the possibilities occur discontinuously. So what exactly does this mean? Let's study Figure 5. After it has been observed (eye of the observer on the far left), the quantum wave expands continually until it collapses as a result of subsequent observing and it disappears and converts itself into a material object at that precise moment. Contrary to the continuous expansion of the wave, this transition happens discontinuously and suddenly. Our conditioning makes it impossible for us to recognize this discontinuity of the quantum collapse. In our ego consciousness, we experience it as continuous. If we were in quantum consciousness, we would have the choice to select from the possibilities—completely unfettered and discontinuously. Once this selection has been made, the quantum waves expand again until they collapse again because of the next observation. This process repeats itself continuously.

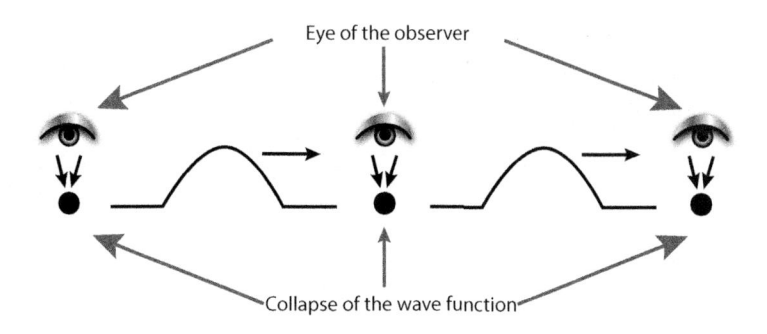

Figure 5: Collapse of the wave function

As mentioned in the previous Chapter, we find ourselves confronted with the problem of dualism. How can intangible consciousness interact with a material world while these two worlds do not exchange energy and signals? This would require the presence of a God, who impacts our world from the outside. If energy were transferred by such an external god, the commonly known conservation laws (e.g. conservation of energy) that have stood the test of time and accrued a proven track record would not be valid. However, none of our experiments so far violated any energy conservation law. We find a way out of this dilemma by presuming that everything is made of consciousness and that therefore quantum consciousness is the foundation of all that is. Hence, material consists of selection options of quantum consciousness. It selects the concrete material and spiritual manifestation from its own options.

Take a quick look at Figure 6, as it will help you envision this process. In it, you will see steps or shadows on a flat surface. Do you recognize both options? If not, try to change your perspective just a little bit. Both of the possibilities inherent in the image—the image of the steps and of the shadows cast by pillars/monoliths—are already present in your consciousness. Do you do anything to the image? Do you have to exchange any signals or energy with the photograph to select the steps or the shadows? No, dualistic interaction is not required in this case because both options already exist in your consciousness. Quantum consciousness (Holy Spirit) uses the same method of selection for the tangible event from the many options the quantum waves (Father) offer.

Figure 6: Stair step or shade profile? Photograph © Karl H. www.fotocommunity.de

Ultimately this means that the world is constantly recreated due to the constantly collapsing wave functions and hence, the recurring selection of possibilities. You might argue that this cannot be true because nothing ever changes in your surroundings. This objection is certainly justified. After all, a table will still sit in the same location even after several hours have passed unless someone moves it. However, if it could be recreated within a fraction of a second as a result of observation, wouldn't it also be possible for an option to manifest itself that recreates the table in a different location? However, that's not the case. How can this be explained?

Do you still recall the Chapter headlined *"What do the terms God and Heaven mean?"* In it, we arrived at the conclusion that something like a godly order exists. It is dictated by the quantum waves. This godly order determines the frequency at which certain possibilities become reality. This also applies to the possibilities where the individual atoms manifest themselves. It is not possible to predict at a certain point in time where the individual atom of a table will materialize. Similarly, going back to the coin tossing example, it is not possible to predict whether the number or the coat of arms will appear on top when we toss an individual coin. However, the atom does manifest itself at the same position—on average, for a large number of observed activities. Just like in the example of the coin toss, we can claim that the coin—if tossed frequently enough—will on average land on the coat of arms or on the number in about half the cases. As far as the position of the table is concerned, there will be minor discrepancies, but they are so tiny that they are not visible to the naked eye. However, these changes in the table's position are certainly physically measurable. Such minor deviations from the computed average also occur in the coin toss example, for instance if of 1000 tosses, 495 land on the coat of arms and 505 on the number.

Quantum consciousness, which we consider the equivalent of the Holy Spirit, thus recreates our world again and again in every single moment. An amazing conclusion! Are there any indications in the Bible that support this statement? Indeed, there are.
Psalms 104, 29-30:
"When you hide your face, they are terrified; when you take away their breath, they die and return to the dust. When you send your Spirit, they are created, and you renew the face of the ground."

The word spirit is used as a synonym for the spirit of God—the Holy Spirit. This means that the world is constantly being renewed and therefore recreated at every moment. The Holy Spirit represents God's power of creation and is congruent with the characteristics we have defined for quantum consciousness. Based on this interpretation, the Holy Spirit constantly chooses from among His own available possibilities the things that will be recreated. However, He is not an entity that is separate from God who makes His choices from the options of a Heaven of the Father that is separate from the Holy Spirit. If this were the case, we would be confronted with the problem previously covered under dualism, i.e. that a transfer of energy and signals would be required to explain the process of creation.

Hence, the only explanation for the creation process—from both, the natural science and the theological perspective—is the Trinity. In quantum physics it comprises the quantum waves, brain-mind and the quantum consciousness; the Trinity of Quantum Physics. In theology, it comprises the Father, Son and Holy Spirit—the Biblical Trinity. Jürgen Moltmann also identified the Trinity as the prerequisite for the process of creation. He writes:

"The Creation exists in the Spirit, it is characterized by the Son and was created by the Father. In other words, it is of God, through God and in God. . . . The fact is that the panentheism, according to which God created the world and simultaneously lives in the world and vice versa, that the world He created simultaneously exists within him, can only be explained and depicted based on the Trinity."

Hence, modern natural science and theology have arrived at the same conclusion.

In Chapter *"What do the terms God and Heaven mean?"* we came to know God as a transcendent entity. Now we have to expand on this statement. Not only is God transcendent—He is simultaneously also imminent. Quantum conscience (the Holy Spirit) is inherent in every tangible object and sentient being on earth because of the creation process described above. Jürgen Moltmann refers to it as imminent transcendence.

You may ponder how something can be simultaneously imminent and transcendent. Once again, quantum physics comes to our rescue as its teaching considers it a given that two seemingly conflicting things exist simultaneously. Quantum objects can be both—particles and waves.

These are obviously two completely opposite characteristics. Waves are vastly expansive and can penetrate each other, while particles are found in one exact location and may collide.

This allows us to arrive at the conclusion that the Holy Spirit is not only the creative facet of God, but also the one that participates in the fate and life story of every human and sentient being. Regardless of the experiences a person has throughout life—positive or negative—God shares the emotions of mankind and "experiences" them with us.

"Hence, in spirit, the Creator is always present in His creation. . . . However, through the presence of His own Being, God also participates in the fate of His own creation. Through Spirit, He suffers the pains of all of His creations. In His Spirit He also experiences the destruction. In His Spirit, he sighs along with the enslaved creature and yearns for relief and freedom." (Jürgen Moltmann, Gott in der Schöpfung).

Consequently, the God we have devised from natural science and whom we find acknowledged by theologian Jürgen Moltmann, is one who shares our joy and our suffering. The Holy Spirit is not a third person who stands between God the Father and human beings and brokers deals, but he is God's personal presence in the lives of human beings.

However, the Holy Spirit also makes it possible for all sentient beings to communicate with each other and with God. "For in him we live, and move, and have our being" (Acts17:28). This communication between humankind and God occurs on a non-local level. No signals are transmitted through space. However, when we converse with other humans, our communication is local and in language that is transmitted to the other person through the air.

By adding the insights we gained in this Chapter, we can now expand our image of God from the perspective of quantum physics as follows:

God . . .
Is non-local in time , i.e. eternal
Is non-local in space, i.e. omnipresent
Is transcendent and imminent
Is the primordial source of all that is
Is Spirit
Means freedom

Means that there is a godly order in our world
Is information
Is alive
Communicates with us all the time
Is the Creator
Is present in His creation and it is simultaneously within Him
Shares the fate of every human and sentient being

Hence, the Bible and natural science agree with each other as far as the quantum waves and quantum consciousness are concerned. However, what is the role of the Son? We will talk about Him more in the final Chapter.

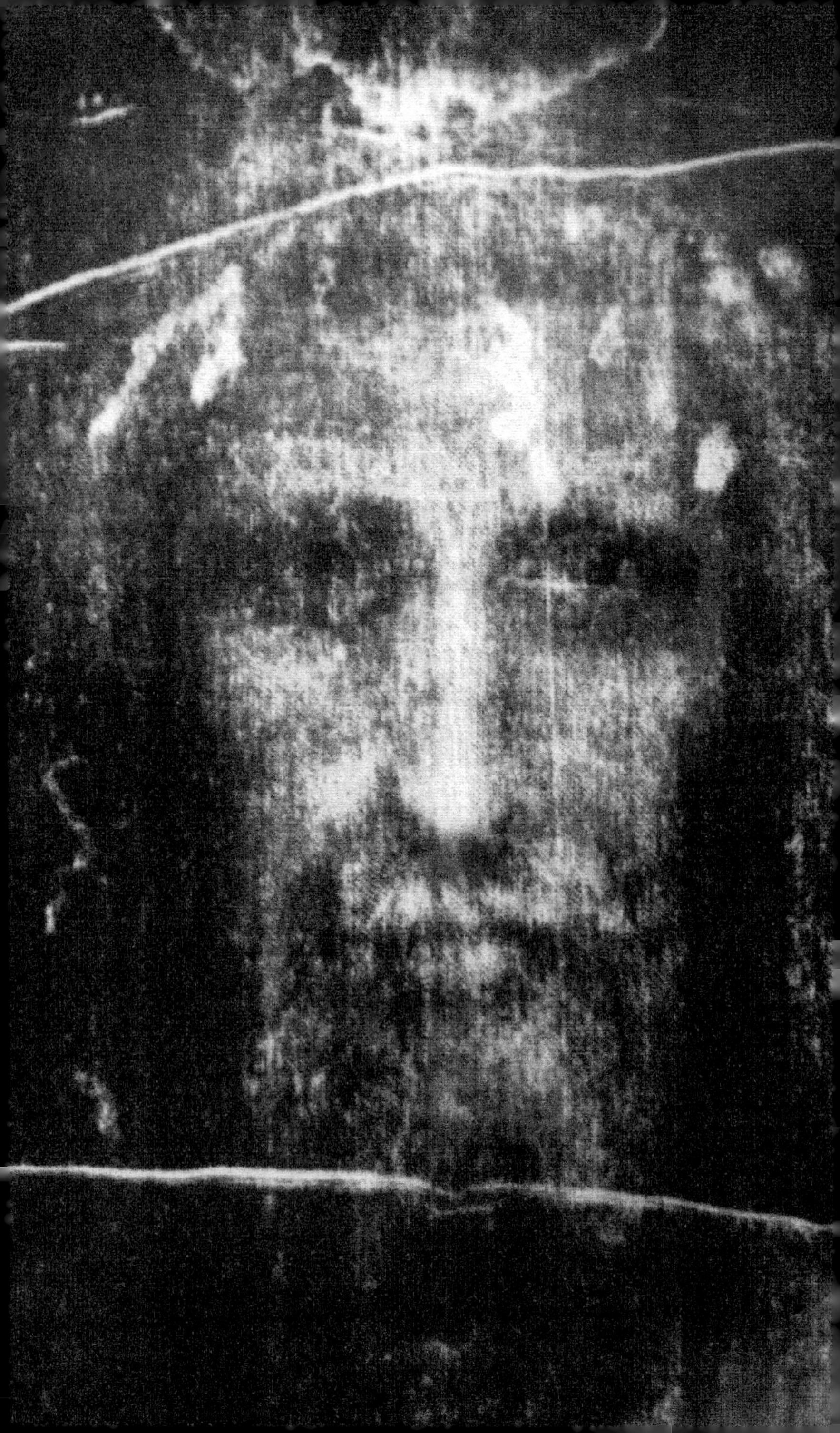

11. Jesus Christ—the Son of God

What kind of life did Jesus live? How did he act? What did he proclaim? Actually, it isn't all that easy to answer these questions since we do not have any written evidence that would have been generated during the era Jesus was spreading his teachings. Historians have identified the New Testament as the only significant source that tells us more about Jesus' life. What is the reason for this? Remember, the first Christians expected Jesus to return at any moment and that this would happen during their lifetime. Hence, initially, they were in no rush to document Jesus' life in writing. It wasn't until Jesus had not returned for several decades and many of those who had actually known Jesus had died that people began to document the story of his life in writing. The Book of Mark, for instance, was written about 40 years after Jesus' death—i.e. about 70 AC, while the Books of Matthew, Luke an John were written over the following 25 years.

In his book *"Der gekreuzigte Gott (The Crucified God)"* Jürgen Moltmann observes:

"But who was the Jesus of Nazareth and what role does he play as far as mankind is concerned? Was he a prophet, who translated the will of God into a language for humans? Was he a savior who brought the blessings of healing all people in need long for? Did he embody God in the world or true human existence before God? . . .

Hence, the sovereign titles do change as the book of faith is translated into new languages and new historic situations. . . . This historic flexibility and variability of the sovereign titles evident in the historic documentation of Christianity, does however have a fixed point and a criterion. It is defined by the proper name Jesus and the story of his life, which culminates in his crucifixion and resurrection. If one wants to define who Christ, the Son of Man or the Son of God is, one has to mention the name Jesus and tell his story. The name Jesus can neither be translated into other languages nor can it be replaced with other names of the names of others. If one wants to say what Jesus stands for, means and does, one has to use the ancient and the new sovereign titles and functional designations; interpret them and complement them with the new ones.

So what does the designation "Son" or "Son of God" mean in conjunction with our newly devised concept

World of quantum waves = Father
Quantum consciousness = Holy Spirit
Material brain-mind = Son

Does this mean that we have to consider the Son equal to Jesus? And is Jesus the Son of God from the perspective of quantum physics?

We have arrived at the conclusion that our material and also our spiritual world can only be explained without contradictions and paradoxes if the intangible wave function (=Father) is caused to collapse by a conscious observation through the one, non-local quantum consciousness (=Holy Spirit) joining forces with a brain-mind (=son). Many of these brain-minds actually exist, given that every human being does possess such an individual awareness. Hence, the term "Son" as defined in quantum physics is symbolic for all human beings—for men, women and children. However, from the perspective of quantum physics there is yet a second interpretation of the word "Son" and it applies specifically to Jesus exclusively and has a very unique meaning. We will talk about this later.

Searching the Bible for indications as to whether completely "normal" people can also be called "Sons of God" or "Children of God," I came up with the following quotations:

Romans 8,14–17
"For those who are led by the Spirit of God are the children of God."

Galatians 4,6–7
"Because you are his sons, God sent the Spirit of his Son into our hearts, the Spirit who calls out, "Abba, Father." So you are no longer a slave, but God's child; and since you are his child, God has made you also an heir."

From the perspective of modern quantum physics, the act of continuous creation can therefore only be explained without contradictions on the basis of a construct of Father, Son and Holy Spirit, whereby every human being is to be viewed as a son—meaning a child—and as someone who is involved in the continuous act of creation.

Leonardo Boff, a former professor of systematic theology, recipient of the Alternative Nobel Prize and one of the most prominent representatives of the Latin American Liberating Theology, also agrees with the teachings of modern quantum physics. In his book *Kleine Trinitätslehre (Short Lessons on the Trinity)* he writes:

"Jesus teaches us that we are also permitted to call God our Father and that as His children, we can consider each other brothers and sisters."

Incidentally, the most popular Christian prayer also confirms this: it begins with the words "Our Father." It speaks of God as the Father of us all.

Consequently, from the perspective of quantum physics, we have a huge responsibility for the wellbeing of all sentient beings and for our world. After all, by participating in the conversion of possibilities into realities, we are involved in the process of creation. By participating in the collapse of the wave function, we affect both, the tangible objects on earth and the quantum waves in Heaven. Every time such a wave collapses, new waves begin to develop, which offers us possibilities of things that may happen in the future. These newly developing possibilities in Heaven are, however, contingent upon the prior collapse of the quantum waves. The Kingdom of God will not become reality until all that is left are possibilities of love—in Heaven and on earth. Based on this interpretation, suffering would not be the punishment of the people by God.

Let's expand a little further on this thought—the thought of what it means to be a son. Given that both, the human body and the human brain consist of matter, the human being, prior to his or her evolution, is already set up as a probability in the Father (quantum waves) based on the quantum physics definition; a scenario that is also described in the Bible:

Genesis 1.27:
"So God created man in his own image, in the image of God he created him"

What exactly does this statement mean? Dr. Hans-Joachim Eckstein, a professor at the University of Tübingen, Germany, offers the following explanation:

"The image is the visible expression of an invisible force, the recognizable embodiment of an invisible entity, the perceivable mirror image of a hidden primordial image."

Hence, we can interpret the word "image" and "visible expression of an invisible force" as a parable for the human being defined as a material manifestation from the world of quantum waves, while the terms "invisible force" and "hidden primordial image" point to transcendent and intangible quantum worlds: The human being as a visible embodiment of the invisible quantum waves (the Father), which can be experienced and resides here on earth.

However, from the quantum theory perspective, we have to expand somewhat on this statement in the Bible, to fully accommodate its meaning. Not only human beings, but also all other things—regardless of whether they are living animals or lifeless objects such as tables—have their primordial roots in the Father. Before it manifests itself, everything within our universe is first established as potential, as a probability, as a primordial image. Every conscious sentient being can therefore be called a son. This is the first meaning of the term "son."

On the one hand, the Bible provides us with terms for human beings—"sons" and "children of God." On the other hand, Jesus is frequently addressed by the name "Christ" or the term "Son of God." How do we interpret these statements? In Mark 8.29, Jesus asks his disciples who they think he is. Peter answers: You are Christ/ the Messiah. The Gospel of Matthew, which was completed later, adds (Matthew 16.16) "The Son of the living God."

Is it indeed possible to reconcile both of these perspectives—all human beings and Jesus are the sons of God? To be able to make a decision, we first have to address the question what the term "Son of God" actually means. Nowadays, we use the term son to designate a biological heritage —a child who was spawned by a father and delivered by a mother. It had the same meaning back in ancient Palestine.

However, another interpretation of the word "son" in conjunction with God did exist back then. The title "Son of God," contrary to the common use of the word "son" was not supposed to refer to biological genealogy, but as a metaphor for the close relationship between God and David as well as the People of Israel. 2 Samuel 7.14: "I will be a father to him and he will be a son to me." In this definition of the term son, the adult King David was not supposed to be a procreation of God, but an adopted son.

The New Testament also contains references to a similar understanding to that evident from the Old Testament. When Jesus returned to shore after having been baptized by John and the Spirit of God (the Holy Spirit) descended upon him, a voice was heard:

Mark 1.11:
"You are my Son, the Beloved; with you I am well pleased."

This story takes it for granted that Jesus was conceived long before that time. In keeping with the tradition of King David, he is being adopted by God as His son and filled with the Holy Spirit so that he can fulfill God's commission.

In this Chapter we have mentioned yet another interpretation of the word "son" in conjunction with Jesus, which I would now like to examine more deeply. I am certain that you have already become accustomed to the "as well as" argumentation thanks to the quantum physics experiments covered by this book. Quantum objects are particles as well as waves. In the case of the term "Son of God" we are also being challenged by such an ambiguity.

Let's review one of the stories about Jesus shortly before the crucifixion. On the way to the Mount of Olives, Jesus tells Peter that the latter will deny him three times that same night. Peter and all the other disciples emphatically refuse to believe it. In the wee hours of the morning, a crowing rooster reminds Peter of Jesus' prediction and he begins to weep bitterly (Mark 14.66–72).

Jesus obviously had the capability to predict the future. From the quantum physics perspective and based on Joseph Ratzinger's as well as Meister Eckhart's interpretations this is in fact an ability to simultaneously be aware of all times. It is, in fact, the characteristic we refer to as non-locality in time and what we have interpreted as the eternity of God. God is in the state of eternity and obviously so is Jesus. Hence, he embodies the characteristics of God here on earth. Jesus is of the same entity as God and if thus defined, he must be called the Son of God. His work is Godly.

We also find examples of Jesus being non-local in space in the Bible—a characteristic we have decided to consider equivalent to the omnipresence of God:

Matthew 8, 5–13:

"When Jesus had entered Capernaum, a centurion came to him, asking for help. "Lord," he said, "my servant lies at home paralyzed, suffering terribly."
Jesus said to him, "Shall I come and heal him?"
The centurion replied, "Lord, I do not deserve to have you come under my roof. But just say the word, and my servant will be healed."

> *Then Jesus said to the centurion, "Go! Let it be done just as you believed it would." And his servant was healed at that moment."*

The healing power takes effect immediately as if there were no distance at all between Jesus and the servant of the centurion. It is exactly like the lesson we learned from the experiments with the entangled particles. As soon as we take a measurement, something happens to the other electron right away. It is as if there is no distance between them. This is the very characteristic of non-locality in space—the characteristic we have come to know as the omnipresence of God, which also appears in the parable of the merchant in the form of Jesus' work. Hence, Jesus has the same impact as the Father (God). He is omnipresent in the world and no geographic distances exist. He is the incarnation of God because the characteristics of God—eternity and omnipresence have taken on the human form in Jesus, as also proclaimed in John 14, 7–8:

> *"If you really know me, you will know my Father as well. From now on, you do know him and have seen him." Philip said, "Lord, show us the Father and that will be enough for us."*

Hence, Jesus is the revelation of God here on earth given that he works in our world in a non-local way in terms of time and space—just like God. Based on this interpretation, modern Christians can indeed believe in Jesus Christ as the Son of God and still be in complete congruence with modern natural science.

Jesus developed an intimacy with God that no other individual had ever been able to establish before and it was characterized by a special closeness to God. Thanks to the Trinity, every person actually becomes part of this special relationship between Jesus and the Father. After all, on the primordial level, from which everything stems, all is interconnected—in a manner that is non-local in terms of time and space. This means that we are not separated from Jesus Christ by time or space—even if he lived in a different country and was crucified about 2000 years ago.

We did not always take a very easy route as we embarked on the journey through this book: from the experiments on non-locality in space and time to the double split experiment, to the interpretation of the results. On our journey we did find numerous correlations between modern quantum physics and Christian faith. Specifically, we were not able to explain the results of our experiments without contradictions until we presumed the existence of a trinity of quantum waves, brain-mind and quantum consciousness. We were able to align this quantum physics trinity with the Trinity we are familiar with from the Bible—the Trinity of Father, Son and Holy Spirit.

As one studies quantum physics, it seems completely unrelated to spirituality. However, the more thoroughly you examine the interpretations, the more natural science and faith have in common. I have an inkling that in the future, other impulses will arise that will uncover further parallels between faith and science. We can look forward to very fascinating times.

About the Author

Physicist Dirk Schneider was born in Karlsruhe (Germany) in 1965. He began to take a keen interest in the secrets of the universe at a very young age and became an active member of an astronomy club as an adolescent. As a young man and student of physics he discovered the links between quantum physics and spirituality. He developed a special passion for this topic and explored the thought processes that are evident in both, natural science and Christian faith. He wrote his book *"Jesus Christ—Quantum Physicist"* after numerous conversations with pastors, natural scientists, theologians and philosophers. It shows how believing in the Father, Son and Holy Spirit can indeed be compatible with a modern scientific worldview.

Visit the Facebook page of non-fiction author Dirk Schneider, which explores subjects related to quantum physics, theology and faith.

https://www.facebook.com/DirkSchneider.Sachbuchautor

Picture credits

Cover, Julián Fidel Marcos Llorente
Diana Sayegh, p. 6, 10, 20, 42, 48, 58,
fotolia 3264040, p. 28
fotolia 9476152, p. 68
fotolia 12372447, p. 82
www.fotocommunity.de (Karl H.), p. 86
fotolia 16439678, p. 92

Printed in Great Britain
by Amazon